Thriving After55

Cover design by
Foster & Foster
1-800-472-3953

Printed in U.S.A.

Attention: Quantity discounts are available for bulk purchases of this book for educational or promotional purposes. Special editions, special covers, or printed excerpts can be created to accomodate your special needs, and the authors are available for speeches, seminars, and workshops. For information, please contact PrimeDynamics, LLC at PO Box 9797, Richmond, VA 23228.

voice: (804) 935-6800
fax: (804) 935=6835
email the authors at:
thrive@primedynamics.com

find **PRIME***dynamics,*ʟʟᴄ on the web at
www.primedynamics.com

Thriving After 55

Your Guide to Fully Living the Rest of Your Life

Henry C. Simmons, Ph.D.
and
E. Craig MacBean

PrimePress
An imprint of **PRIME***dynamics,* LLC
Richmond, Virginia

Excerpts from *Out of the Skin, Into the Soul* by Dorothy Albracht Doherty and Mary Colgan McNamara, copyright © 1993 reprinted by permission of Innisfree Press, Philadelphia, PA. 800-367-5872
Excerpts from *Daily Bread* by Marc Kaminsky, copyright © 1982, published by University of Illinois Press, Urbana, IL, reproduced with permission of the author.

Publisher's Cataloging-in-Publication
(Provided by Quality Books, Inc.)

Simmons, Henry C.

Thriving After 55 : your guide to fully living the rest of your life / Henry C. Simmons and E. Craig MacBean. — 1st ed.
p. cm.
Includes bibliographical references and index.
LCCN: 99-91366
ISBN: 0-9668813-1-1

1. Middle aged persons—United States—Life skills guides 2. Aged—United States—Life skills guides. 3. Retirement—United States—Planning. I. MacBean, E. Craig. II. Title

HQ1059.5.U5S56 2000   305.24'4
                                       QBI99-1607

First printing November, 1999

10 9 8 7 6 5 4 3 2 1

∞

To all of you who,

in your length of days,

have shown us

the promise and possibilities

of living long and thriving.

You may not know who you are,

but we do.

And we thank you

for gifts without measure.

∞

∞

Acknowledgements

There are many people who have contributed to this book. We acknowledge and thank them all.

Special thanks to Thos and Diane Leonards, Josie Sicheri, and Helen McDonald for their unending encouragement and support. This would not have been possible without you.

A deep nod of appreciation, also, to Caryn Summers, our editor. Without her contributions this would not be the book it is.

Finally, we acknowledge each other as co-authors. Looking back over the iterations and incarnations of this manuscript, there is hardly a sentence that we can identify as coming from only one or the other. Co-creation isn't always easy, but this has been great fun—and now we can hold each other responsible, in big ways and small, for ideas and how they are expressed.

∞

Table of Contents

Introduction

Aging happens.

And, with advances in various technologies, it happens to more people every day.

It will probably happen to you.

How it happens is a variable, maybe *the* variable, and your experience of aging is up to you. We would like to empower you to engage aging without either succumbing to it or trying to overpower it. We wish for you the experience of the possibility of living your life fully and thriving—right to your last breath. Only those who accept the reality that they are aging day by day, who confront the possibility of frailty and the inevitability of death, have the wisdom to plan for, and the courage to embrace, the rest of their lives with exuberance.

You have choices, of course. You can deny aging, or try to control it, but that is ultimately a losing proposition. When people age, control is exposed as a false idol. Or, you can just succumb to aging and let it happen on its own terms. That is less satisfactory since, left to happen on its own terms, aging in America can be outrageously and unnecessarily expensive. That price is measured in the profoundly human currencies of psychological pain and spiritual agony, as well as in dollars and cents. The impact of it is widespread and indiscriminate. Your entire community of support—spouse or partner, children, siblings, friends—pays along with you.

It does not have to be that way.

To age can mean to live long and to thrive. Your thoughtful choices now will profoundly shape the rest of your life, and determine whether you fully live it or merely survive it.

The practical steps to paying for a longer life—in all currencies—are grounded in the answers to three questions. There is no right answer to these questions, except the answer that is right for you. You need to answer these questions in ways that will work for you.

The questions are:

- ✦ Where will you live?
- ✦ How will you pay for it?
- ✦ How will you live?

Your answers to the first two questions will help you deal with the practical matters that are the context for thriving. Your answers to the third question address your habits of body, mind, heart and soul. These are the domains in which thriving occurs. The answers will help you to keep and to deepen what works to affirm life, and to add more supportive options to replace habits that would otherwise undermine your thriving. These choices will enable you to determine how fully you live the rest of your life.

As you live through all the phases and stages of aging, including the likely circumstance that you live long enough to grow frail, four things will be so:

- ✥ The place where you live will support your living;

- ✥ The financial resources you need to support your living will be in place;

- ✥ Any frailty care you need will be given in the setting you have chosen; and

- ✥ Regardless of any physical limitations, your ways of being with yourself and others will work to enhance your quality of life and thriving.

Rather than experiencing this as a time of desperation, defeat and tragedy, being "a little further up the mountain" may be a time of psychological well-being and spiritual completion for you, for those who love you, and for those whom you love. You *can* live fully, right to your last breath.

But none of that will happen without preparation. Making plans and taking action five years too soon is preferable to trying to scramble when it is even five minutes too late. This book is about making conscious choices *now* about where you will live while you age and how you will pay for what comes up during aging—both in coin of the realm and in more profoundly human currencies.

THE FLOW OF THIS BOOK

Here, in Section One, we start by exploring aging with a survey of some recent cultural attitudes toward growing old. You will see here that some of those attitudes—if left critically unexamined—can work against your best interests.

Then we lay out a method of understanding the process of aging that gives you a context for making choices. This is a common sense picture of the likely patterns of life from middle age through dying. With this understanding of the phases and stages of the unfolding of your life, you can make choices about living a longer life on terms you can live with.

This is achieved by answering the first two strategic questions, "Where will you live?" and "How will you pay for it?" In this case, "it" represents the economic expenses associated with aging, such as having something to live on when you are not earning an income, and paying for help if (when) you need frailty care.

You will also need to build foundations of character and strong habits of the heart, body, mind, and soul to empower you to fully live the rest of your life. This is done by answering the third question, "How will you live?" These three questions, their answers and your choices, are the subjects of this book.

SECTION TWO: WHERE WILL YOU LIVE?

There are only five possible answers to this, the first strategic question. We call these choices HOME SWEET HOME, THE FAMILY PLAN, THE LAST RESORT, THE NEW FRONTIER, AND

PROGRESSIVE RETREAT. We devote a chapter to each answer. In these chapters you will learn what we mean by each choice and explore the dream behind it. Then you will look at the pros and cons and explore the issues surrounding each one. You will find that you already have preferences, values, interests, and questions. This section will help you to clarify your thinking and to make an informed choice.

SECTION THREE: HOW WILL YOU PAY FOR IT?

In this section you will learn how to assure yourself of financial security throughout aging. In order to do that, you will need to distinguish between retirement income planning, frailty planning, and estate planning. Those planning processes are best thought of as developing answers to these three questions:

1. If you stop working, what will you live on?

2. When the time comes, how do you want to be cared for and how will you pay for frailty care?

3. When you die, what will happen to those who depend on you financially, and to your estate?

Each of these types of planning involves complex issues and interactions, but all of them have three elements in common. In each kind of planning, you will have to deal with:

a. What you want to have happen;

b. The information you need to make that happen;

c. The technical expertise to implement the plan.

In retirement income planning (1a), "What do you want to happen?" has to do with whether and when you will want to replace the income that comes from working for a living with income that comes from money working for you, or benefit plans. Frailty planning (2a) has to do with where and how you want care to be given if or when you can no longer function independently. In estate planning (3a), "What do you want to have happen?" has to do with taking care of people (or institutions) who depend on you economically, as well as what you want to happen to the things and wealth you have accumulated.

The information you need to know for retirement income planning (1b) is about what income streams will be available to you from benefit plans, and what assets you will have that can be put to work to generate income.

The information you need to know for 3b—estate planning—is very similar, but focuses on different aspects of some items.

The information you need for frailty planning (2b) is less about your specific situation and what you have and owe, and more about what resources are available to help you pay for the support and care you will need when you become frail.

In Chapter 10, *False Hopes: the Taxpayers' Money*, we look at Medicare and Medicaid and how they may or may not support you. In Chapter 11, *Deep Pockets: Your Money*, we look at how home equity conversion and life insurance restructuring may provide an unexpected resource for funding frailty care. In Chapter 12, *Shared Risk: Other People's Money*, we explore long term care insurance as a choice to eliminate the possibility of frailty wiping out your retirement income and estate plans.

Finally, there is the issue of getting expertise to implement your plan. Technical expertise is unique to each case and situation. We will not try to make you an expert, but will recommend how to find an appropriate professional (or professionals) to help you.

SECTION FOUR: HOW WILL YOU LIVE?

Fully living the whole of life is a function of more than having a roof over your head and feeling financially secure. In Section Four we explore the profound impact of character on the quality of life in old age. The answer to the question, "How will you live?" deals with how you relate to your self and to others. Unexamined ways of expressing self and relating to others developed in the first half of life won't necessarily work as your life unfolds to its completion. You will explore thriving in the contexts of body and mind in Chapter Thirteen, and heart and soul, or spirit, in Chapter Fourteen.

Throughout the book you will find spaces to express your own insights, questions, hunches, and conclusions. Forget what you learned in first grade about marking up books! It is important that you make notes as you go along so that you have a record of how you got yourself to the conclusions at which you arrive.

Thriving After 55 is about making choices now, and about getting ready to live a longer life than any previous generation, and about being prepared to fund the rest of your life in all currencies. We hope you find it to be a good read. But more, we hope it will help you to make life-affirming choices. Life is too long to do otherwise. We cannot promise great longevity, but we do offer you the possibility of thriving to your last breath, no matter how long you live. We invite you to live fully and to grow old gracefully, starting with the preparations you make here and now.

Editorial Note

Throughout the book you will find us referring to "you and your spouse" or "you and your partner." Partner here could refer to a life partner to whom you are not legally married, for any one of a number of reasons. It could also refer to a sibling, or a friend, or someone else with whom you have made a commitment to share resources. We do not mean to make any political statement by these references, but rather to recognize reality.

CHAPTER TWO

The Measure of Your Days

Aging hasn't always been the way it is now. Well into the 1900s, few people reached age 65. Most succumbed to disease in childhood or early adulthood. Around the turn of the twentieth century, it became widely accepted that diseases were caused by germs. Germ theory led to improved personal health care practices, such as boiling bottles and milk, washing hands, protecting food from flies, isolating sick children, and ventilating rooms.

Physicians were the first to implement these practices in their families. By 1924, the mortality rate of physicians' children was 35% below the national average. The mortality rate for children of teachers and other professionals declined as rapidly. Public health officials aggressively disseminated the germ theory to an eager audience, and death by childhood disease dropped sharply.

In the 1940s, the development of antibiotics represented another major medical breakthrough with equally beneficial implications for longevity. By the middle of the century, infectious diseases had been essentially brought under control.

With all this, there was a dramatic shift in the number of people living long and reaching retirement age. Because of the advances in sanitation and hygiene, and also advances in medicine, pharmacology, fitness, and nutrition, people born from the middle of the twentieth century on have come to expect to live well into retirement and to die of degenerative conditions, rather than of trauma or infectious diseases.

The trend toward longer living creates a new set of challenges. Past generations worried about the possibility of dying young and leaving economic dependents. This generation faces a different quandary: departing in slow motion and becoming an economic and emotional burden on their children and society.

In 1935, the year Social Security came into being, less than one percent of the population had a pension plan. People worked as long as they could. When they could no longer work, they lived on whatever savings they had. When money ran out they moved in with one of their children, if they had children surviving, or into the poorhouse. Within a few months, maybe years, they died of some infectious disease, often pneumonia—"the old person's friend."

Today, people retire expecting to go on living a very long time, maybe as much as a third of their lives. They know— you know—that these can be very good years. But you also know that long life is likely to be a mixed blessing. The longer you live, the greater the likelihood of frailty. The longer you live without working, the greater the possibility of running out of money. The probability of living longer and dying slower and poorer casts a dark shadow. These realities are close to home for many of you as you watch your parents, or the parents of close friends, grow old—many of them on terms not of their own choosing.

Many adult daughters and sons of the generation that lived through the depression and fought World War II won't "abandon" their parents in their old age, and are paying the price of the failure of an older generation to prepare for something that they could not have foreseen. As you watch this happen, be reminded that the costs of frailty are paid by many people, and be aware that you can no longer claim to be taken by surprise.

From Chronononsense to Conscious Aging

What we seem to know about aging in our culture doesn't always make a lot of sense. It is often chronononsense—that is, nonsense about the passing of time and growing old—mostly because aging is cast in either all positive or all negative terms.

You get messages every day about what it is like to get old in America. On the positive side, you hear messages that successful aging is staying young. You learn from TV and printed advertisements and sources such as the magazine *Modern Maturity* that the old are just like you—only wealthier, with more time to enjoy life, and maybe with some gray hair. They garden or play golf every day and the sun always shines on them. Viagra™ seems to have solved the problems that may once have been part of being old.

On the negative side, you get messages—often from politicians—about old age as a time of poverty. You hear that the old need to have their dignity restored, implying that age has stolen it. Aging is pictured as an existence to be endured either in dismal nursing homes or as a burden on the next generation. Cocktail napkins and bumper stickers tell you to "Get revenge—live long enough to be a problem for your children."

We went to a large bookstore recently and asked one of the store's pleasant (young) employees if there was a section on aging. She promptly pointed us to the "Health and Fitness" section, where we found a couple of dozen books about never getting old. We also found a book about Medicaid Planning, and a few books about taking care of your aging parents.

Looked at together, these messages tell us that aging is either about staying young, or it is about living death. These are overstated positives or overplayed negatives. The way aging is portrayed in our culture reflects the enormous value that is placed on looking young, being strong, being productive, and being in control. In doing so, the culture disconnects old age from living, and encourages you to discredit a rich and vital phase of your living.

Human At Any Age

During the adult working years you are trained to segment the various aspects of life. You talk about your business life, social life, family life, religious life, personal life, and so on. Time management books and seminars challenge you to make goals in each of these areas, and then to balance them. Life is seen as a juggling act that requires strength, agility, and enormous energy to force reality to conform to your needs so that you can achieve your goals.

The dark side of this segmentation is that it allows you to ignore what you don't want to deal with. The segmentation process, unchallenged, leads you to put off preparing for old age, because the unspoken assumption behind the process itself is the vigor of youth. Segmentation leads you to imagine your life without its last years and breeds a subtle but devastating denial. This denial of old age is sometimes called the Cleopatra Syndrome (Cleopatra is, after all, the Queen of Denial).

The last third of life offers the opportunity to integrate the various dimensions of your one life, while living fully right to your last breath. The last third of life—aging—can be the richest part of your span of years. Beautiful young people are accidents of nature, but beautiful old people are works of art. You are most likely to become a work of art if the last third of your life is lived on a stable foundation, and seen as a part of a life that started not at retirement, but at birth.

The fact of the matter is that life is given as a whole. You are an infant, then a child, then a teenager, then a grown-up. You are middle aged, then an older adult, and then a very old (and possibly frail) adult. Successful living means thriving and living fully, no matter what your age, right through the last of your days. Successful living is not limited to the sterile vision of being young until you are very old, and then dying without engaging any of the inevitable changes of living long.

Dying young at a very old age may be what we all say we want, but it is not an option. The notion of living young and dying quickly is a modern fantasy. In this fantasy, the perfect death comes painlessly in your sleep, at home, the night after you have won your club's Seniors Golf Championship. The only thing acknowledged as old is the wine at the celebratory dinner of gourmet food you shared with your closest, completely healthy and hearty friends! It might happen that way—for a very few. In a time in which the signs of aging are to be hidden if they cannot be fixed, the blessing of age is rapidly reduced to its potential for leisure and consumption.

At every age, no matter what the culture wants us to believe, you are capable of being fully human and fully alive. Old age, even frail old age, is not an inhuman time of life. At age 120, Jeanne Calment said, "I dream, I think, I go over my life, I never get bored." When the culture caricaturizes the successful old as those who never age, it sets you up to devalue something that is truly beautiful—the exquisite human qualities of character in the very old.

When you look at the old as unique human beings, you see that they are no less people now than they ever were. In many ways, some of those who are old and thriving are more fully persons than they ever were because they are so little concerned with pretense, and committed to savoring the day, expressing themselves, and reaching out to others. They are *present* in the world, not merely passing through. They may be closer to death than you are, but they thrive in part because they accept death as an integral part of life.

There may be aspects of their lives that are not as pleasant as they would wish, but in their minds and spirits they understand that this is their one and only life, and they are *living* it.

From the outside, you may judge the quality of a frail life as poor. But when you actually engage the people who are there, you find that they are often quite delighted with the quality of this day. You can never wisely judge the quality of another's life from the outside. If you try to, you wind up missing the character of the person living that life.

LIVES IN PROGRESS

One of the ways that aging is caricaturized is to collapse life into good years and bad years. A life in progress is never that simple. Phrases such as "Go-go, Slow-go, No-go" or "Hale elderly, Frail elderly" do not take you very far in understanding the challenges and delights of thriving beyond middle age. Like all of life, periods of stability and times of transition mark the last years.

Understanding this and distinguishing these stages and phases of aging helps you to engage the whole of life in your "life in progress."

When does aging begin? No one can say except by looking backwards, but everyone is sure that it is sometime after "middle age." James Fisher, a colleague and friend, has developed a way of talking about getting older that has been very helpful to us in this regard, although we have modified it somewhat.[1] Try this, and see if it helps you to include aging in your thinking about your one and only life.

Our model distinguishes three stable periods, each followed by a transition. If you were to draw a picture of them it might be a continuous squiggly line:

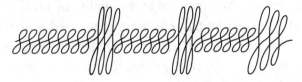

This diagram suggests that even the calm or more stable periods of life can be quite eventful—with lots of ups and downs, twists and turns, and ins and outs. The diagram also suggests that there are brief, intense transitional times of life that turn our worlds topsy-turvy. After these transitions, life never goes back to just the way it was before.

We name the periods of stability and the transitions by highlighting one feature characteristic of each. Thus we call the first period of stability EXTENDED MIDDLE AGE. Aging is connected to a life already in progress, and is not isolated from that life. To reinforce this thought, our diagram should really be drawn like this, with the dashed part of the line representing middle age:

READY OR NOT   LIKE IT OR NOT   DYING

MIDDLE AGE   EXTENDED- MIDDLE AGE   THE NEW ME   THE REST OF LIVING

How long EXTENDED MIDDLE AGE lasts can not be predicted. It could be less than a year, or it could be ten, fifteen, or more years.

We call the first transition READY OR NOT, since no one is ever really ready for the dramatic kinds of changes that mark an end to EXTENDED MIDDLE AGE—changes that might include the death of a spouse or a personal debilitating illness. READY OR NOT is shorter, more intense, and often more dramatic than the periods of stability on either side of it.

The second period of stability is characterized by THE NEW ME. You cannot stay in the turmoil of the previous transition; you must pick up the pieces of your life and build a new identity. As with EXTENDED MIDDLE AGE, the duration of this period is as varied as the number of people who live through it, and can last for few or many years.

Inevitability marks the second transition: LIKE IT OR NOT. This is the transition into frailty and dependence. Contrary to conventional wisdom, it is relatively brief—a year or less, usually—but it is intense and life-changing.

This transition, too, ends in a period of stability. We call this last stable period THE REST OF LIVING. It is a time when you will probably have limited mobility (hence REST) but—also contrary to conventional wisdom—you will still be capable of expressing yourself and reaching out to others in new ways (hence LIVING). Again, how long this stable period lasts is unpredictable, but it can go on for many years.

The final transition we call, simply, DYING. Taken together, these three periods of stability and three transitions make up aging.

In our diagram we have not indicated the length of these periods of stability and times of transition, or the likely age of onset. Those are unpredictable variables. In the last third of life, chronology (that is, how old someone is) tells us very little about a person. You might be in THE NEW ME in your early sixties if EXTENDED MIDDLE AGE is cut short by a tragic accident or a difficult transition to retirement. You might also still be in EXTENDED MIDDLE AGE at 80, or even 90. We know one pair of identical twin sisters, now age 74. One of the sisters regularly runs marathons, including Boston. The other is in a nursing home with a degenerative disease that requires constant medical attention.

In the last third of life, knowing the age of a person gives no useful information about the state of the person's life. Conversely, saying what stage a person is in explains a great deal. Someone in THE REST OF LIVING (at whatever age) has needs that arise from dependency, while someone in THE NEW ME lives with entirely different issues.

Knowing about these stable periods and transitions will help you to understand why developing answers to the questions, "Where will you live?" and "How will you pay for it?" is so important to fully living the rest of your life. It is, after all, *your* life, and the extent to which you are prepared to deal with its twists and turns will determine the extent to which you are able to thrive no matter what stage or transition you find yourself in.

EXTENDED MIDDLE AGE

✀ Harry* retired as the most senior accountant in a large company. For the next several years, with the same routine with which he had gone to work for decades, he now goes to work with a group that calls itself Associated Senior Executives. Harry often talks about how deeply satisfying it is to help small business owners get the best advice possible about starting a company or handling their personal finances. No casual observer would ever notice his successful transition to EXTENDED MIDDLE AGE. ✀

EXTENDED MIDDLE AGE begins when aging is acknowledged publicly, usually by Medicare or Social Security eligibility. It is often difficult to observe any substantive changes from middle age. For many people, one difference may be the absence of children in the home.

Typically, the beginning of this period coincides with the end of a career, and may be referred to as "retirement." However, the two should not be confused. People in EXTENDED MIDDLE AGE are often engaged in lifestyles with activities that are difficult to distinguish from the lifestyles of "40- and 50-somethings" who are definitely *not* retired. For some, what will be different is the absence of the rewards and demands of structured work environments. But for others, working will continue without change or interruption. Still others will choose to redirect their efforts to non-income-producing activities, but without a decrease in energy or commitment.

---

*All names have been changed to preserve the anonymity of the real people whose stories are told in this chapter.

The period of EXTENDED MIDDLE AGE is marked by a continuing sense of control alongside intimations of frailty. It can last a very long time. In the context of the question, "Where will you live?" this is the period with the fewest complications and the most options. Be mindful, however, that choices about where to live made in and for this period have major consequences in later phases and stages of life. From a financial perspective, this is the period of life people usually have in mind when they talk about or do retirement planning.

The challenge of EXTENDED MIDDLE AGE is to understand what it means to live responsibly in the context of aging, and to prepare for what lies ahead while living joyfully in the present. This period may be the last chance you will have to consciously grow into the person you want to be for the rest of your life.

READY OR NOT

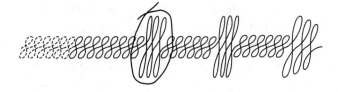

   ⅋ *Margaret was a friendly, open, gregarious neighbor to everybody she ever met. Everybody knew Margaret, and Margaret knew everybody, because she was such a great conversationalist. One day, a sore throat seemed to slow her down a bit, and when it did not get better a visit to the doctor revealed a tumor on her larynx.*

*Following a long and difficult recovery from surgery,
she had to learn to talk by holding a sound generator
to her throat. Conversation became a major effort, and
both Margaret and her family and friends struggled to
adapt to her new—and very different—reality. Many
people said they hardly even knew her any more.* ஒ

Typically, EXTENDED MIDDLE AGE ends in a transition that we call
READY OR NOT. The hallmark of this transition is a loss that
requires a significant change of lifestyle and/or a redefinition
of your self in the light of changed circumstances. Such losses
are most typically the death of a spouse, the deterioration of
your own physical well-being, or the deterioration of the physical or cognitive well-being of your spouse or partner. This
transition may come at any age—although the longer you live,
the closer you get to its reality.

There can be no certainty when READY OR NOT will happen,
or even that it will. Some people go right from EXTENDED MIDDLE
AGE through LIKE IT OR NOT to THE REST OF LIVING, or even straight
to DYING, although advances in life-support technologies
make this increasingly unlikely.

As noted, what often marks READY OR NOT is a dramatic
event like the death of a spouse, the loss of good health, or the
need to change where you live. Whatever the specifics, what
triggers READY OR NOT is that something happens that is
beyond your control, and you are forced to redefine who you
are relative to the world around you. This task is not often
undertaken consciously in our culture, and so skills are likely
to be either insufficient or nonexistent.

The challenge in this transition is just to stay on your feet—emotionally, spiritually, physically and financially. You must now make choices about a new lifestyle and self-identity, perhaps for the first time in over half a century. Those who are attached to notions of control may find these new waters especially rough.

READY OR NOT is when decisions about where you will live in aging begin to have significant consequences. Both community and convenience translate to sources of support for you in the transition process. Moving during READY OR NOT can be especially traumatic. If the loss that initiates this period is the onset of a chronic, debilitating illness—physical or cognitive—the cost of care for special needs can be a significant addition to your budget. Such additional costs almost certainly will go on for the rest of life.

Finally, choices you have made, either consciously or unconsciously, about how you will live can be felt especially strongly in READY OR NOT. The extent to which your image of your self is tied to your physical well-being will be a significant factor in how you handle this transition. You are more likely to do well here if your mental habits are flexible than you will if you are stuck with certain behaviors that have not changed in decades. A person who has reached out to others in need is more likely to find critical support and help than one who has not. A sense of spiritual relatedness can provide an anchor in a stormy sea. A life lived in a one-to-one relationship with the sacred will provide a foundation for self-expression, and a source for the generosity to embrace others in this transition and right through to your very last breath.

THE NEW ME

❧ *Victoria's husband, Charlie, died suddenly just months after he retired. Following a period of grieving that she barely remembers, Victoria began the process of building a new life.*

She took classes in personal finance so she could learn how to handle the money Charlie had left her. The person with whom Charlie had worked on their investments seemed patronizing, so she found a different advisor, one with whom she was more comfortable.

She decided to "start life over." For the first time ever Victoria was faced with deciding where to live and considering what she could afford without Charlie's help. She looked ahead, sold the house she and Charlie had lived in for more than thirty years, and moved to a life care community where her bridge partner lived.

Victoria continued playing bridge as she had when Charlie was alive, but now she also felt free to travel widely—something Charlie had never liked to do— with a new friend she met at dinner.

Victoria feels good about her new life, and how she has handled making decisions. She is enjoying herself,

> *and making new friends. You might say she has*
> *become a new person, and is thriving in her new envi-*
> *ronment.* ∾

There is no going back. Following the READY OR NOT transition one has to pick up one's losses and build a new and satisfying life based on a new reality and self-identity.

Whatever the trauma of the transition, you adapt to the extent possible. For example, instead of being Mrs. John Jones, you are now "Widow Mary Jones" and you travel on pre-packaged tours, instead of freelancing with your husband. Or, instead of being either Bob or Harriet Dale-who-are–both–healthy–and–can–go–anywhere, you are now one half of a couple adapting—often surprisingly well—to the restrictions of a wheelchair. Or, you are John Carver, and you have given up your regular golf foursome and resigned from your volunteer responsibilities at church because your wife needs your attention day and night since her stroke.

Whatever the new set of circumstances, and no matter how it constrains your freedom or how much it impacts your finances, in order to get on you will need to embrace your new reality. Of necessity you will have to forge a new lifestyle around that reality. While you may be the same person inside, your circumstances have changed dramatically. For some, this period is difficult; the transition never seems to end. For many, the adaptation to THE NEW ME is remarkably positive. For all, the process is individual and can continue for years.

In the context of the question, "Where will you live?" the notion of moving now may be either supportive of—or disruptive to—a new sense of self. From a financial perspective, this is a period where it is possible to create a lifestyle based on whatever the economic situation is, although the facts of any special needs will impact that lifestyle dramatically. The challenge here, and it is a significant one, is to live creatively past one's losses and within one's limits. If you have not undertaken to do so already, this is the period where you find that it is necessary to refine old habits of the body, mind, heart and soul, or create new ones.

LIKE IT OR NOT

John's mom died first. That wasn't the way it was supposed to be, but that's what happened. At first John and his wife, Jean, were concerned for Gus—John's dad—because his mom had handled so much of the day-to-day running of the house. After a few months, that concern faded as Gus seemed to tolerate his NEW ME *status pretty well. He learned to cook some simple things so he could eat when he felt like it, and played some golf, and followed the stock market on CNBC.*

John and Jean went back to focusing on their careers. After a couple of years, during phone conversations, John sensed that his dad was maybe starting to "lose it" a little.

At Thanksgiving, John and Jean came to visit from the east coast. They were shocked to see how dirty Gus's house was, how confused he seemed from time to time, and how many unpaid bills there were stuck in books, magazines, and disorganized desk drawers. John found that his father hadn't balanced his check book in over six months. What had been a vague concern from 3,000 miles away became a living horror.

At first, Gus was reluctant to even talk about moving out of the house he had lived in for so many years. Later, after his daughter-in-law had gone home, he was able to confide in his son, "I guess it's for the best. Sometimes I am terrified that I will become completely disoriented when I'm driving and hurt somebody. I don't want to be a burden on you. Will you help me to decide where to go?" ∽

The onset of LIKE IT OR NOT is signalled by your loss of physical health and mobility or notable deterioration of your mental faculties. This transition marks the change from THE NEW ME (or maybe directly from EXTENDED MIDDLE AGE) to THE REST OF LIVING. It is a personal passage into dependence. No one likes it, but some handle it better than others.

What happens is this: either your body or your mind ceases to function adequately for you to get along in the world without assistance. Resistance to dependence is ultimately overwhelmed by the grinding reality of not being able to make it on your own. Now, you need to be in an environment where you can get the help you need for daily living.

In the context of the question, "Where will you live?" this is when choices have significant consequences, since the inability to care for yourself requires an environment that will provide that support. From a financial perspective, this is when "How will you pay for it?" begins to take on special significance, since your increasing inability to care for yourself requires someone else to fill that role. There will be a cost for that, measured in dollars and cents or, perhaps, the more precious currency of a friend's or relative's vitality.

This transition need not signal the death of the spirit or the capacity to live fully, but the challenge is to accept one's limits and to prepare to live in dependence with dignity. The transition is often traumatic; much of what you have prized all of your life slips away. The habits of body and mind that define self, and of heart and soul that motivate relationship to others and to the Divine, will be tested. To live life fully in this period means to attach great significance to small accomplishments and gestures.

THE REST OF LIVING

∞ *Sam has been a nursing home resident for six years. He needs assistance to get out of bed, to get*

> *dressed, and even to eat. He is completely dependent on the staff.*
>
> *So what is his concern? He needs one more vote to be reelected President of the Residents' Council. He rings for help to get wheeled down to work the Day Room. There, he thrives—fully alive in the process of hearing grievances and suggestions, and soliciting the votes he needs to put him "over the top."* ∞

This last stable period is potentially rich and engaged, but it is also a time of dependence and frailty. From the vantage point of the middle years, it is the period of life most of us fear. Along with LIKE IT OR NOT, this is the period we associate in conversation with "getting old." As to where you will live during THE REST OF LIVING, your needs for both assistive and medical support, and community, are preeminent. That these services are not free is self-evident.

The response to THE REST OF LIVING is unique for each individual. For some, this is a period of resignation and loneliness. For others, a new environment can bring an opportunity for contentment. There are inevitable losses, but there are also possible gains. The gains can be precisely in the quality of life. What does quality of life mean in this context? It means being fully alive when that cannot be expressed as physical fitness. It means being engaged with others when that cannot be expressed as clever conversation. It is most easily seen in the lights of your eyes, where the spirit dances when the body no longer can. It means being loving rather than self-pitying, and reaching out to others rather than being self-absorbed. It means going with the flow of life rather than bitterly cursing your inability to control it.

The real challenge in this period—which can go on for many years—is to continue to express yourself and relate to others despite your limitations. There will be diminishments, but your humanity need not be diminished. This is the period where the habits of heart and soul developed earlier in life, and refined or reformulated in EXTENDED MIDDLE AGE and THE NEW ME, will be the foundation of your living. This is where patterns of character based on love rather than fear will pay great dividends.

DYING

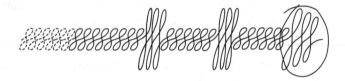

❧ *Sheila was dying, and she knew it. Nobody else wanted to accept it, and they went around saying encouraging things to each other. Sheila told her daughter that if they didn't stop, she would amend her will to have her tombstone engraved, "I told you I was sick."*

Her greatest desire was to be conscious and present right to the end of her life and to die naturally without medical intervention except to relieve pain. This was Sheila's parting gift to those who were able to face the reality of her eminent death with her.

> *Even Sheila's young minister took courage from his*
> *visits to her. At her memorial service, he said that he*
> *had learned from Sheila more of what it really means*
> *to have faith. Since her death, many of Sheila's friends*
> *celebrate the completion of her life with the strength*
> *and joy they have borrowed from her dying.* ∾

The final transition we call, simply, DYING—but death is not simple. For virtually all of human history this transition has been seen as the culmination of life, as a religious event to be prepared for with one's whole heart and soul. Well into the twentieth century, the public prayers of some Christian denominations routinely included a plea to be delivered from a "sudden and unprovided for" death.

But this is not the mood of our times. We live in a secular age, and even death is often removed from the religious domain. Nonetheless, for many DYING is life's last sacred act. But dying is more than just an end; it is a profoundly human event. The quality of DYING is enormously important and will have a deep and lasting impact on the people who love you. The challenge here is to make DYING a fully human act.

Recent research by Dr. Daniel Mroczek and his colleague, Christian Lolarz, of Fordham University, and Dr. Laura Cartensen of Stanford, has found a positive correlation between aging and a heightened sense of well-being. As reported in *The New York Times*, these researchers found that the older the respondents were, the more likely they were to experience positive emotions like cheerfulness, good spirits, and happiness.

How about you? Do you expect that you will be happier—or less happy—ten or twenty years from now?

Give yourself a moment... which of the phases and stages of life that we have described are you in now?

[ ] MIDDLE AGE

[ ] EXTENDED MIDDLE AGE

[ ] *READY OR NOT*

[ ] THE NEW ME

[ ] *LIKE IT OR NOT*

[ ] THE REST OF LIVING

[ ] *DYING*

Where (in which period) do you think it will be easiest for you to experience positive emotions?

What period are you most afraid of?

What period do you most look forward to?

What other thoughts or fears have come up so far?

What questions do you have now that you hope will be answered?

¹James C. Fisher, "A Framework for Describing Developmental Change Among Older Adults," in *Adult Education Quarterly*, Winter, 1993.

SECTION TWO

Where Will You Live?

In Section One we established a basic vocabulary for thinking in creative and realistic ways about the journey of life all the way through aging. This next section is about a practical yet sophisticated approach to making one of three critical choices in planning for your journey.

The three critical choices are framed as questions:

- Where will you live?
- How will you pay for it?
- How will you live?

Certainly, all three questions interact. You may not even let yourself think about some possible answers to "Where will you live?" because you judge that strategic resources (such as money) are not available. Likewise, the answers to "How will you live?" will profoundly influence your choice about where you will live. A person, for example, who places exceptional value on community might make different choices than a private individual. Similarly, the availability of certain payment options for care—for example, long term care insurance—may influence your housing choices.

All that being said, "Where will you live?"is still the first question we invite you to consider. The answer you choose deeply influences the whole rest of your life. We humans are very physical, bricks and mortar kinds of beings. Place is a significant part of self-definition. Home is not only where you hang your hat, it is also, in part, how you know who you are. The choice about where you live sets your path. The further you go along your path, the more it diverges from paths not taken. Beginning with this question will help you discover, in personal, emotional, and even passionate ways, some of your deepest values, needs, and loves.

Where, then, will you live? At a strategic level, there are only five possible answers. We will deal with each of the five individually. Each of them is an equally valid choice, but only one of them is the best choice for you. For each possibility you will find a definition of the choice and an articulation of the dream scenario behind it. You will walk through the pros and cons, and consider the issues that you will need to deal with if you make that choice.

At this point *Thriving After 55* takes a personal turn, because you will find yourself attracted to—or repelled by—one or another of these options, perhaps passionately. Most people have strong but unexamined convictions in this area. If you and your spouse or partner don't share the same convictions, you may find yourselves challenged by the process.

This challenge may be because you had not previously considered all of the choices. For some people, such an apparent oversight about something so important can be unsettling. If you find yourself challenged, it may be because you realize that the choice you previously decided upon may have been viewed through rose-colored glasses. That is to say, you may feel confronted if you come to realize that your first choice only makes perfect sense in the dream scenario.

This is where the process of considering the pros, cons, and issues must be both personal and objective. Personal—because it is your thriving that is at stake. Objective—because this is a question that needs to be handled in the bright light of reality. The process should also be empowering. Good, sound planning will produce a supportive reality, and that must start at home.

CHAPTER THREE

Home Sweet Home

WHAT IT IS

By HOME SWEET HOME we mean the decision to stay in the house you (or you and your spouse or partner) already occupy for the rest of your life. Implicit in this choice is the notion that you will rely on people coming in to help when either or both of you go through the LIKE IT OR NOT transition and can no longer function independently. Sometimes this choice is expressed as, "They'll have to carry me out of here in a wooden box."

THE DREAM SCENARIO

What is the dream behind this strategic choice? It is that you will live comfortably in the home where you have lived your life, and your long-time friends and community will support you. If you grow frail you will have the help you need, and you will die gracefully in your sleep in your own bed.

Your home may well be the most perfect embodiment or expression of your self. Most people put a very personal imprint on the place they live—that is how a house becomes a home. Memories get hung on the walls and woven into the fabric of the house so that they ultimately constitute a part of who you are. Over the years you collect your "treasures;" things are arranged in certain ways so they are comfortable for you. The furniture becomes part of you; even old scuffs and marks are familiar parts of your landscape. Home is a place where you live out a familiar and comfortable rhythm of life, cooking and eating, talking and resting, sharing love and living.

There are other familiar parts of the home landscape: neighbors, stores, places to walk—all real parts of the self, building blocks of your reality. The club you belong to or the congregation in which you worship is part of the fabric of home. The alley or street where you raised your children brings back fond memories. The garden that matures with you is part of who you know yourself to be. Why would you ever want to leave this place?

The notion that you will continue to be strong enough to take care of this old house that has become your home is also part of the dream scenario. After all, you have taken pride in caring for it, and you know a plumber and an electrician. Even if you can't do as much as you used to, or do it as quickly, you know you can cope!

Lastly in this dream scenario, if you get sick, you will go to the hospital where you are known and come home to build your strength. You have been healthy here a long time; you will continue to be healthy here. If it is absolutely necessary, you will have people come in to help—and when the time comes to die you will die in your sleep, at home, in your own bed, surrounded by your family.

No wonder this is a preferred strategy. The dream is wonderful! We all know a few examples of people who have lived this dream. We hold on to them dearly. Those people stayed in their home to the very end and did, in fact, die in their own beds.

Such dreams are part of our unconscious in-scape, of our personal realities. Now, let's bring this up to a conscious level and look at the pros and cons. In the bright light of day, what is at stake?

THE PROS

As a conscious strategy, there is not much to distinguish the pros of HOME SWEET HOME from the dream scenario:

1. The home you live in is familiar, and familiarity breeds contentment. You know your way around—how many steps to take to get to the couch; where the bathroom light switch is; what all those sounds are in the middle of the night. This house is home, and a "senior moment" of forgetfulness won't be quite as disorienting as it might be in a new place.

2. The neighborhood is home, too. You know how to get where you are going, you know what lane to get into to make your exit from the expressway smoothly, you know where the barber and beauty shops are and where to take your shirts so they are done the way you like them. You may already be an active member of a congregation or social club; people recog-

nize you on the street; every face is not a stranger's face. You know your doctor and dentist. You can write a check without showing your ID. Getting through a day doesn't take a lot of conscious energy.

And, not least, you know who and how to help. It's your turf. You need not be defensive—it is more likely to be your role to welcome the newcomers and initiate them into the rhythms of your community. In short, you are part of the community of support.

3. Home is an economical, "right" place to live. You have already spent the money and energy to make it yours. If you have paid off the mortgage (or even if you haven't), it may seem like the cheapest place to live. The big money is already spent. You have made the house into what you want it to be. You can enjoy the money you have already put into it that you know you would never get back on a resale.

You have decorated it to your taste, you have planted the flowers you love, and the tree you planted as a sapling is at last the shade tree you wanted. You have learned to live with the house's imperfections and idiosyncrasies. When the kids come to visit, they have a place to stay and stories of their childhood home to tell their children—your grandchildren.

4. You don't have to move. Nobody wants to move. It is not fun. We see signs for "Adventures in Moving" on the side of rental trucks, but we know better. Open-heart surgery is also an adventure, but…

Staying in your home is the only non-disruptive option.

Take a minute here, please. Put the book down and try to identify someone you know who aged this way, whose life may be the raw material of *your* dream. Make a note of who that person is—or who those people are.

If Home Sweet Home is your strategic choice to answer the "Where will you live?" question, it will be worthwhile to check with others who knew the same person or people you identified to see if their memories are as warm and happy as your own. Others may have seen reality somewhat differently...

THE CONS

These are the possible negatives to choosing HOME SWEET HOME as the answer to "Where will you live?" as you age. Careful attention here can help you to keep HOME SWEET HOME from becoming Home Bittersweet Home.

1. Who you are can become inseparable from this particular structure. All your sense of well-being can be invested in your house. The home may be the most perfect expression of

the self—but it is not the self. It is possible to get to the point where you cannot imagine yourself apart from this house, where your house speaks for who you are, so you can't speak for yourself. In that case, your motto has become, "I live here, therefore I am." It sneaks up on you; it is part of the slow motion departure of aging.

2. The neighborhood may shift around you. The kids who cut your grass and shoveled your driveway have houses of their own now—in another neighborhood. The minister that made you feel at home has retired, and the replacement does not know your history with the church. Your doctor has moved to Arizona. Stores come and go; what you used to be able to purchase on Main Street you now have to go to the mall to buy. Distances grow. Before, the library was only a quick trip; now it seems like a major expedition. Traffic patterns change and there is no way to exist in most neighborhoods without driving.

The people who move into the neighborhood may not be "your kind of people." Kids sound louder than they used to, and their cars or motorcycles and music are noisier than you remember cars and motorcycles and music being when you were younger.

3. Your house is uneconomical and the "wrong" place to live. What was home for the whole family is now too big for you. You rattle around in the place. In moments of clarity you wonder why you have all this space. The location of rooms is inappropriate: second floor master bedrooms and basement laundry rooms don't work well for you any more. Houses with steps to every level are difficult for people with walkers. Bath-

rooms with 28" wide doors are neither wheelchair-accessible nor walker-friendly. Showers and bathtubs without grab bars are dangerous.

Heating and cooling, painting and other routine maintenance get very expensive, particularly relative to a fixed income. Energy and skill levels sink: what would have been a weekend chore is now a nagging nightmare that won't go away, a constant reminder of your limitations. Taking care of your house, once a joy and a point of pride, can become an insurmountable challenge.

When the kids come to visit, they have to do what you can't do. They have to come to visit because you need them to do your chores! This robs both of you of the chance to talk and share and enjoy each other's company.

4. The decision to stay in your home rests on the assumption that things will never change, at least not too much, but that is not real. What if you wake up one morning and realize that moving is simply beyond you—that you no longer have the strength, the courage, or the wherewithal to go somewhere else? The home of your dreams has become your prison.

When the decision to go or stay is no longer up to you, someone else may put you somewhere. It will be extraordinarily difficult to make that place your home. If you think a couple of pictures on the wall or photos beside your bed will make it home, think again. It takes focused energy to create a home from a physical space.

The Issues

If HOME SWEET HOME is a choice you want to consider further, you need to carefully think through the following issues:

1. Be very careful to distinguish between house and home. A house is a physical structure; a home is a place in the mind and heart, and what you make of the space in which you live. Think back to when you moved into your house and it was empty. What you could see in reality was a physical structure, with its beauty and its flaws. What you saw was a house filled with life and happiness, all the people and things you loved. We all have a little bit of the romantic artist, Norman Rockwell, in us, and we tend to see our houses through his picture-perfect American-as-apple-pie eyes.

The strategic issue here is to strip away the Norman Rockwell image that confuses house with home and look at the reality of the house and the neighborhood and the community you live in. The journey from *Better Homes and Gardens* magazine to the Century 21™ sign in the front yard, from glossy dream images with fuzzy edges to the stark, hard-edged reality of how a prospective buyer will see your house is difficult, but it must be made.

2. Be aware of the potential cost to your spouse or partner if that person becomes your caregiver. The impact of caring tasks can cause intense stress, and lead to physical and psychological problems for the caregiver, particularly as she or he is also likely to be experiencing some of the diminishments of aging. Caregiving may well be a labor of love, but it will certainly be a labor.

3. People are discharged from the hospital sicker and quicker these days. Be aware that the health care system increasingly expects intimate medical procedures to be performed at home. Often, home procedures will not only require intimate care, but also physical strength. Will the physical layout of your house help or hinder this, whether you are living with a partner or by yourself?

4. Be aware of house maintenance issues. If a house is not going up, it is going down. A house is made of bricks and wood and pipes and wires and paint and shingles and heating and cooling systems—all of which deteriorate with time. Maintenance can be ignored or deferred for only so long without jeopardizing the integrity of your house, and with it your safety and well-being. You need a consistently implemented program of preventive and routine maintenance. Costs and the availability of trustworthy workpeople become critical issues.

5 Consider issues of remodeling or retrofitting. Can your house be modified to meet new needs that come with aging, at a price that makes sense? Can you put a ramp up to a door? Can an elevator be added? Can hallways and doorways be widened? Can bathrooms be made accessible and safe?

6 If you are living with a partner, plan for a future when one of you has died. Will the decisions you both make in EXTENDED MIDDLE AGE still work for one of you in THE NEW ME? Are you setting the survivor up to fail? Will the house you treasure together be a place that is suitable for one of you alone? If not, how much harder might a change be later?

7. How will this strategy hold up through all the phases and stages of aging? Will it be as good a choice in THE REST OF LIVING as it is in EXTENDED MIDDLE AGE? What assumptions have you made—perhaps unconsciously—and what will you do if those assumptions don't come true?

8. Sometime early in EXTENDED MIDDLE AGE, some people choose to set up a new house. This is often a move to a more favorable climate. It may also be a move to a retirement village that is not a Continuing Care Retirement Community (CCRC). You will learn much more about CCRCs in *The Last Resort*, but the issue here applies to retirement housing that does not provide supportive and health care services. With the exception of the pros and cons of moving, or the grandkids visiting, what is relevant for HOME SWEET HOME also applies to retiring to a new place and setting up home there.

HOME SWEET HOME is, for many of you, a very attractive first choice. Your excellent planning and thoughtful consideration of the issues can help turn the dream that stands behind it into reality.

❦

A Thoughtful Exercise

In your gut, right now, do the pros of Home Sweet Home outweigh the cons? Or, do the cons carry more weight? Try to list your strongest reactions:

1.

2.

3.

4.

5.

What does your spouse or partner think? Does he or she have the same opinion?

If you have a spouse or partner, do the two of you share the same dreams about what aging will be like and look like, where you will live, what you will do? If not, how do you differ? If you are single, what is your dream?

CHAPTER FOUR

The Family Plan

WHAT IT IS

When we talk about THE FAMILY PLAN, we mean the choice to move in with one of your children and her or his family when (or before) you can no longer function independently. It is a decision to rely on your children to shelter and care for you when you can no longer care for yourself—if it ever comes to that. Sometimes this is expressed as, "My kids will take care of me (just like I took care of my mother or father)."

THE DREAM SCENARIO

What is the dream scenario behind this choice for life-sustaining housing? It is that, when the time comes, you will live comfortably in the home of one of your children, where you will share warm companionship, pool economic resources, and be together as a family. If you grow frail, your daughter or daughter-in-law will take care of you, and you will die gracefully in your adopted home surrounded by your children and grandchildren.

This dream is part of the self-reliant, independent American dream of the frontier (as interpreted by 1950s Westerns), when the extended nuclear family was all that people had. It is a dream born in an age when the issue of survival was real to everybody and there was no government safety net. In that era, which many now view as a golden age, even the most frail expected to have a place in the family. People died at home, and quickly. Taking care meant simple human compassion, and no one was abandoned to the poorhouse. This dream has a strong moral component, which is expressed in different ways. Some say, "This is what families are for;" others claim, "We take care of our own." Some quote scripture—"Honor thy father and thy mother;" others are more biological than theological and are guided by the notion that "blood is thicker than water."

This dream is cast in a language of right and wrong. THE FAMILY PLAN is part of an assumed, unspoken commitment that when the going gets tough, your family will be there for you. It seems a natural part of family life—you are responsible for those who are helpless whether they are your young or your old. If you can't take care of yourself or yourselves, someone in the family will be there to help.

Implicit in the dream scenario behind THE FAMILY PLAN is that taking care of your family is not a burden, and when you pull together it's good for all of you. It is a dream fuelled by memories of stay-at-home mothers and grandmothers who took care of the oldest and frailest members of the family, in the family home. It is a dream of days when you went upstairs to visit Granny or MawMaw after school and of the happy times you spent in her room. It is the payback for parents helping children to get started in the world.

Lastly, it is a dream that comforts the husband in knowing that, "When I die, Mom will be taken care of."

This is a wonderful dream. When it works, it embodies the very best of American family values.

THE PROS

1. If you choose THE FAMILY PLAN strategy, you can share deep human relationships with those you love. You will continue to experience the richness of family until the end of your life. Your sense of identity as part of your family will continue if your spouse dies. Your grandchildren will grow up knowing you, and will learn your values. The family story will not be lost; rather, it will be woven into the lives of new generations.

2. The pooling of assets and resources should make life easier. Financially, it costs little extra to keep one or two more people in the house. Even an in-law suite or a granny cottage costs less than a whole separate residence. Pooling financial resources might allow the family to move to a better home. Logistically, there are more people to share the tasks of running a household and raising a family.

3. Informal caregiving is built in. Grandparents who are not yet into LIKE IT OR NOT or THE REST OF LIIVING provide safe, loving, trustworthy babysitting. When the children are of school age, there is someone at home after school to supervise

them, and transport them to their activities. When they are teenagers, there is someone there to monitor with whom they go out and how they spend their time.

4. On the other side of that ledger, when you grow frail someone will be there to help you with the tasks of daily living that seem beyond you, from writing checks and driving to the doctor's office to helping you dress or bathe.

There will always be someone at home to assess and respond to your changing health status. Those who love you will see that you have the health care you need, that the best preventive measures are taken, and that you follow through on treatment. If you need hospitalization, you have a home and family to return to. If you need facility-based care, you will make the decision with input from those who know and love you best.

THE CONS

1. The list of negatives for THE FAMILY PLAN strategy begins with psychological or behavioral considerations. The level of interpersonal skills required to succeed in this venture is enormous. You have likely not lived with each other for an extended period of time as adults. You will be moving into an established family with its own established dynamics; it is not possible to move in without making an impact. Every member of the family has to have the skills and the commitment to redefine roles, values, lifestyles, intimacy, and authority relationships.

If you get past this first hurdle you are still not on solid ground. In a culture that prizes personal growth over stable relationships, families are inherently fluid and potentially volatile. Grandchildren grow into teenagers; parents are constantly redefining who they are in their relationships with each other and their children; you will make new demands on the family system just by being there.

If for any reason it doesn't work and the household breaks up, the emotional cost of disentangling yourself can be enormous. If family relationships deteriorate, you can find yourself in an emotional crossfire—blamed, victimized, or permanently excluded. Relationships with adult children often only work at arm's length. In the closeness of one house, the natural hurts and resentment of growing up may fester and erupt.

2. Practical considerations must be examined next. Is the physical structure of the house going to work to support you living in it with your family? Will you and the family have appropriate privacy? Who will set the house rules? Who will be in charge or control when disagreements arise? Can the house be modified to accommodate walkers or a wheelchair? Who sets the thermostat and determines how bright the lights ought to be? Is your room soundproofed against your grandchildren's music—or can it be? Who chooses the channel on the TV? Is there enough space to park another car?

3. There are also financial considerations. The risk in the pooling of financial resources is the complete loss of your investment, or contribution. The fact that you have moved into a son's or daughter's home probably means that you have disposed of all or most of your furnishings. About one in five American families moves each year: people get job transfers,

people get ill, people get laid off, and people go through rocky times in relationships. People separate or divorce and break up their own households.

To start over again as a householder may be beyond your financial capacity. You may have made an irrevocable commitment of your financial resources to help purchase a better home or build an in-law suite; how will the value of this be measured now—potentially many years later? Disentangling yourself financially may leave you with severely diminished resources, particularly if you do not have a formal, legally binding agreement.

4. The demands of built-in child care can be a trap. When you are well and active, you may not want to be tied down to unlimited baby-sitting obligations. The charm of grandchildren for many is that you can give them back to their parents! To the extent that you are "domesticated" you may not be able to enjoy the kinds of social relationships, activities, and contacts that will contribute to your own thriving.

Values change greatly from generation to generation. When a grandparent has primary responsibility for childcare, there is an almost inevitable conflict between the grandparent and the parents over how the grandchildren/children should be raised. These dynamics are complex; the parents of the grandchildren are still and forever the children of those same grandparents.

5. The demands of caring for a parent may have dramatically negative consequences, especially for the daughter or daughter-in-law. Most jobs and careers do not allow unlimited leave for parent care; many do not allow any. Even sym-

pathetic employers have production requirements to meet. If the caregiver has or can arrange for a telecommuting job, or a home-based business, the constant interruptions that go with caregiving can be an even greater problem. Working at home needs even more concentration than working at work. Because it is an unstaffed job, or business, there is always more that needs to be done.

If one of your children or children-in-law has to quit her or his job to care for you, the economic and personal impact can be staggering. Economically, there is lost income, pension, and Social Security credits. Benefits will be lost, too. For many, loss of spousal medical benefits is intolerable (a lot of women work primarily for medical benefits for the family). For the person leaving a job, there is the loss of a sense of contribution, of freedom, of social contact, even of self-worth. Caring for you may replace some of these, but it is not likely to replace all.

Women who care for older disabled relatives because it is their duty—rather than as volunteer or paid caregiver—state that it causes intense stress and psychological and physical problems. One article referred to theirs as "half lives." Marital tensions have often been kept below the surface by the relative freedom of both husband and wife at work. Forcing one or the other to stay home for parent care (no matter how much a labor of love it may be) will eventually expose these tensions. Similarly, resentments or unresolved issues between parents and children—let alone husbands and wives and parents-in-law—that were held at bay by distance and separate households may become exposed.

6. The prospect of being bathed by your son or daughter or son- or daughter-in-law, or having them change your diapers, is seldom considered when the decision is made for you to move in. As the nations's health care system continues to narrow its focus on acute episodes of illness, informal caregivers at home are required to perform intimate medical procedures that were only done in hospitals by trained medical personnel as recently as the mid-1990s.

7. No one gets into an arrangement like this knowing how long it will last. We know one woman whose mother-in-law came for the weekend—and stayed for 33 years. She stayed through a move from the midwest to the southwest when her son retired, and through her son's death, and through more than ten years of her own REST OF LIVING period.

Deep breath.

Before you despair of THE FAMILY PLAN, list for yourself what attracts you to this possible choice.

1.

2.

3.

What are the cons that seem most surmountable?

1.

2.

3.

Is there anything that just seems impossible?

The Issues

If The Family Plan is an option for you, you and your family need to consider these issues:

1. Everyone who is involved needs to be part of the negotiation about whether or not this is an appropriate choice. This is fertile ground for the law of unintended consequences, as we see in this cartoon:

© Lynn Johnston Productions, Inc./Dist. by United Feature Syndicate, Inc.

From the beginning, every party that has a stake in the arrangement needs to communicate face-to-face. Although friends may be a second tier of stakeholders after family, their connectedness to the person must also be considered. In the cartoon above, not only is Grandpa leaving his home to move to someplace far away, he is also leaving friends—some of whom may have counted on him deeply as part of *their* community of support.

What is an appropriate process? This is the piece that often gets shortchanged, perhaps because it demands honesty and open communication. It will probably be best done over several days or weeks. It will be emotionally charged. There may have to be time to resolve old hurts.

First, gather the stakeholders together with an impartial outsider. This might be a trained counselor, a perceptive clergy person, an arbitrator, a family systems therapist, or perhaps an empathetic lawyer.

Second, lay out all the possible options and all the consequences and circumstances you can anticipate. Possible circumstances include (but are not limited to) divorce, job loss, job transfer, illness or death of adult children, and the precedent this move sets for other family members. After all, if you move in, why shouldn't your son-in-law's or daughter-in-law's mother or father move in, too?

Third, make the best possible decision that everybody can support. The focus now is no longer *exclusively* on what is best for you, although any decisions that are inherently bad, such as "musical houses"—having your children take turns housing you—must be precluded. Every stakeholder must support the decision. One disaffected party is likely to upset an otherwise balanced boat, now or in the future.

Fourth, hold off implementing the decision. Let it simmer for four to eight weeks. The decision to leave one's own home—with all the meaning we attach to home—and to become part of another home, with all the disruption unavoidably attached to that, must be taken slowly. Changing the decision at this point is much less painful than having to undo a done deal.

2. Obviously this strategy demands a high level of communication. Keep in mind that the issues are emotionally charged and often touch the realm of the taboo. Absolute truthfulness about any history of abusive relationships or substance abuse is mandatory. You must also talk about bathing, toileting and diapering, and we don't mean what brand of soap to use or whether the toilet paper should come off the roll from the top or bottom. How does everybody feel about having to do it to you or for you? If you can't talk about it, you shouldn't plan on having them do it—and they shouldn't agree to do it.

3. If you decide together that THE FAMILY PLAN is the best possible strategy, then all agreements need to be worked out in detail and put in writing before the move is made. If that does not happen, preconceived, unarticulated, biased, and conflicting memories of verbal agreements will rule your roost. An agreement that is not a good agreement for everyone is a bad agreement for everyone. If (for whatever reasons) all parties are not willing to detail the agreements in writing, then you should not consider this option further.

In these written agreements you need to:

a)   Protect the economic interests of all parties, as to both contribution and return. How much should you contribute towards renovation or acquisition of a bigger house? How much should you contribute to the family budget? If you need more care than your children can give, or are willing to give, who pays for it?

If the arrangement stops working, even after all that preparation, your financial rights have to be protected. If you have sold your home and broken up a household, how can you begin again? Your son's or daughter's rights also need to be protected. The possibility of financial hardship can put enormous pressure on your family to continue arrangements even when they are psychologically destructive.

b)   Specify the obligations and authority relationships among all the parties. Who has final authority; whose rituals will be observed; who sets the household rules; who disciplines the kids/ grandkids and how; what forms of discipline are OK and which are off limits? If you want to date will you be free to do so? Can you stay out overnight without getting everybody upset? Is it OK for you to be absent for extended periods? Will you be expected to go on vacation with the family? What vacation arrangements will be made when you are frail?

c)   Work out procedures for emergencies and make sure all legal authorities are in place. If you are expected to act as a caregiver for your grandchildren, you will need written authorization (and you will need to be able to find it). You will also need to give your family a general Power of Attorney and Medical Power of Attorney, with Advanced Medical Directives.

d)   Make explicit decisions about the level of care that you expect your family to provide, and what the next steps will be if and when that care level is exceeded. Include who the arbitrator will be if there are disputes. It is quite possible that you will reach a point where the level of care that you need can only be given in a facility-based setting by paid staff. It often happens that adult children caring for a parent with

Alzheimer's disease move the parent to a care facility six months too late. This is understandable, given the potential emotional tangles, unless there are prior agreements for an outside arbitrator to help in the process.

e)   Prepare "review and exit" strategies. What works on day 100 may not work on day 1,000. The economic interests of your grandchildren for education might compete with your needs for care. Your child's family relationship may fall apart. If people who agree to live together "until death do them part" can split up, who is to say that even the most thoroughly negotiated agreement for housing and care for your lifetime won't be broken?

4. The ability to retrofit or modify a home needs to be taken into account. The same issues that we detailed in *Home Sweet Home* apply here.

THE FAMILY PLAN has worked and is working very well for many families. Properly prepared for and thoughtfully approached, it can be a fine choice. Excellent planning with your family can help you turn your dream scenario into a lived reality.

A Thoughtful Exercise

In your gut, right now, do the pros of THE FAMILY PLAN outweigh the cons? Or, do the cons carry more weight? Do the issues seem real to you? Try to list your strongest reactions:

1.

2.

3.

If your only possible choices were HOME SWEET HOME and THE FAMILY PLAN, which would you choose?

[   ] HOME SWEET HOME   [   ] THE FAMILY PLAN
Why?

This is one of those "spaces to express your insights, questions, hunches, and conclusions." It is important that you capture your thoughts and feelings in their white-hot, uncensored form. Have at it!

CHAPTER FIVE

The Last Resort

WHAT IT IS

THE LAST RESORT is the strategic choice to relocate to a Continuing Care Retirement Community (CCRC)—that is, to a community with common dining facilities, support services, and shared resources for recreation, education, and health care—at a time when you are still healthy, active, and functioning independently. With one decision, one contract, and one move all future decisions about where to live, regardless of health status, will be taken care of. This choice is sometimes expressed as "I'll never be a burden to to my family or friends."

Our name for this choice, THE LAST RESORT, has drawn strong reactions. People who live in—and therefore understand—CCRCs object to the implication that these communities are something "to be resorted to."

Others think that to speak of these communities as resorts in any sense is to glorify them inappropriately. These people tend to have impressions of CCRCs as nursing homes. That is to say, their experience of a CCRC has been limited to people who moved into or moved their parents into a CCRC during the LIKE IT OR NOT transition or in THE REST OF LIVING period when they needed significant levels of care. This is not a fair evaluation of CCRCs as an answer to the "Where will you live?"question, but it does reflect a widely held misunderstanding.

Some clarifications about Continuing Care Retirement Communities are in order. By definition, CCRCs are retirement communities with on-site facilities for long term medical care and assisted living. CCRCs are communities. They are places where people share life together and support each other at one level or another.

The level of luxury varies widely from one CCRC to another, and is usually reflected in the entrance fee (which may or may not be partially refundable) and monthly fees. These fees cover personal dwellings, common facilities, and shared resources, although the extent of health care facility coverage varies from CCRC to CCRC and by payment structure.

There are three basic payment structures for health care facilities behind the entrance and monthly fees in CCRCs: "extensive agreement," "modified agreement," and "fee for service." Typically, any one CCRC will utilize only a single payment structure, although we know of some where you can choose. The difference between the three types of payment structures is the extent to which the actual use of assisted living and health care services is reflected in the normal monthly bill.

✦ *Extensive agreement payment structures* have monthly fees that stay constant regardless of the level of care you get. CCRCs using extensive agreement payment structures usually have significant front end and high monthly fees, although they are not necessarily the most luxurious facilities. CCRC residents with this kind of agreement get unlimited—but specified—health services. For example, some CCRCs have Alzheimer's facilities or programs, and others do not. Monthly fees are the same for everyone in the same type and class of dwelling, whether you are using the health care facilities or not. Thus, the financial risk of a prolonged episode of intensive health care for any individual is spread among all the residents of the community, even in the case of a disease like Alzheimer's.

✦ *Modified agreement payment structures* have fees that will be lower than extensive agreement fees, all other things being equal. Like an extensive agreement plan, modified agreement plans provide both assisted living and nursing care with no change in fee, but only to a pre-determined extent (e.g. a total of 30 days of nursing care). After that pre-set limit, extra costs are passed through to the resident on the basis of usage, and reflected in that individual's monthly bill. However, because of the up-front fee and shared risk, the costs of actual usage are likely to be lower than comparable nursing care or assisted living costs outside the community.

✦ *Fee-for-service agreement payment structures* do not include any assisted living or health care services in the regular monthly fee. Thus, when these services are utilized, the full cost is reflected in your monthly bill. Again, the costs of actual usage, because of the up-front fee and shared risk, are likely to be lower than comparable nursing care or assisted living costs outside the community, but responsibility for paying these costs is entirely yours.

Regardless of how residents pay for these services, access to appropriate levels of care is generally guaranteed to all residents of a CCRC. In a world where Baby Boomers may well overwhelm available resources, this is not an insignificant benefit.

There is one additional consideration. Many CCRCs refer to themselves as "life care communities." Under California law (at least), a CCRC can call itself a life care community only if there is a guarantee that if you are a resident and run out of money, you can't lose your residency or your benefits. That means that you would have to be financially subsidized by the community or its backers. We have found no other state in which the designation of "life care community" is anything more than marketing language. Let's face it, "life care community" sounds better than "continuing care retirement community" or "CCRC"—but the same guarantees may not exist elsewhere.

Regardless of payment plans, these communities are diverse. They range from high-rise apartment structures to expansive campuses on large acreages, and from fewer than 100 residents to over 1,000. The residences may be apartments, townhouses, duplexes, clusters, cottages or detached single family structures. Floor plans in CCRCs vary from studios and one bedrooms to two and three bedroom units, and even larger. CCRCs can be found in urban, suburban, and rural areas. They offer different services and programs, but common to most are shared dining rooms, activity and exercise areas, and some form of outdoor recreation. All of them make provision for health care on site, excluding acute care (hospitalization). Entrance fees range from under $100,000 to well over $500,000, and monthly fees from under $1,000 to more than $4,000.

REALITY CHECK

When you think of THE LAST RESORT, are you dealing with your own preconception of Continuing Care Retirement Communities? It might be in your best interests to visit two or three CCRCs just to get some sense of what they are really like.

Contact the American Association of Homes and Services for the Aging (AAHSA) and order a copy of *The Consumers' Directory of Continuing Care Retirement Communities*. The cost is $30 plus $3.50 shipping and handling. Call AAHSA's toll-free publications number, (800) 508-9442, to place your credit card order or, if you are calling from the Washington, D.C. metropolitan area, call (301) 490-0677. You also may fax your credit card order to (301) 206=9789 or mail your order to: AAHSA Publications, Department 5119, Washington, DC 20061-5119. It is a reference book that will be very helpful.

THE DREAM SCENARIO

What is the dream scenario behind THE LAST RESORT? It is that you can consciously decide to make a new home in a place in which everything you need will be taken care of as long as you are alive. It is borne on an attitude that even if you can't control aging, you can outsmart it! This choice is often expressed as, "I will never be a burden (especially to you kids)."

You will enjoy your golden years in appropriately designed structures and a mutually supportive environment. When you go through the LIKE IT OR NOT transition, you will have the help you need and will remain among friends who understand your situation, and who can visit you easily. You will die peacefully, with the best care and support possible.

People who make this choice prize their ability and willingness to make appropriate decisions about the whole of their lives. To make this choice is to look aging squarely in the eye and make the decision that the best place to live the rest of your life is in a community specifically designed and set aside for older adults to live and die.

"Living in community" is the key phrase. These are facilities built around active lifestyles and being with other people. Residents share amenities such as workshops, craft rooms, computer rooms, libraries, health club facilities, game rooms, rooms for movies and dances, swimming pools, tennis courts, walking trails and direct access to golf courses. In some ways, these places are truly resorts, complete with activity directors who bring in speakers and organize educational events, recreational events, travel, and religious activities. What makes it possible to provide all these facilities is that the resources are shared. What only the richest could afford individually, residents of a CCRC can enjoy together.

Among the like-minded and similarly situated residents of a CCRC, there is a high level of mutual understanding, awareness, and support. People are not only inclined to look out for each other, but their physical proximity—particularly in the common dining room—facilitates mutual attention and care.

Another positive aspect is the presence of medical care. People who choose to move to THE LAST RESORT while the going is still good face the negative prospects of frail old age—and preempt them. They make sure that all contingencies are planned for ahead of time. They understand that THE REST OF LIVING and DYING need not be a terrifying burden. They make appropriate choices for the kinds of chronic and terminal conditions that often accompany old age. For them, nursing facilities are not an all-or-nothing choice but simply part of a continuum and community of care. In a CCRC it is not uncommon for people to spend a period of time in nursing care designed to help them recover, and then return to the lifestyle they never really had to leave.

Many people who choose to move to their LAST RESORT see this decision as the best gift they could ever give their children. They have made judgements about the kind of care that they are likely to need and have opted for their needs to be met by professionals. They have made what they see as a realistic assessment about exactly what their families will be able to do for them when they are sick or dying—that is, not to provide hands-on care, but rather to give the loving gifts of presence and support.

Lastly, in this dream scenario, THE LAST RESORT is the best possible community of support for a surviving spouse. Here there will be people who understand. There are systems and structures that are more permanent than life itself, and the survivor will have friends with whom to engage in activities and a wonderful base from which to spend time with family.

No wonder this is an attractive strategy. It takes the least benign view of old age and, with an alchemist's skill, turns the dull gray lead of frailty into the bright gold of life in a caring community. This is a gift for both yourself and for those who might otherwise have had to give care.

THE PROS

1. Moving to a CCRC is a package deal. You will live with like-minded people in a community designed for safety and security through EXTENDED MIDDLE AGE and beyond. You don't have to search for recreational, educational and avocational facilities, or for a place to go for dinner or people to go with. When you need a heavy object lifted or the lights put on the Christmas tree, there is someone to call to help. When the time comes, neither you nor your children will have to shop for assisted living or nursing care. Regardless of your state of health or where you are in the stages and transitions of aging, this place is your home and your monthly cost of living is fixed, subject only to annual cost-of-living increases and utilization of health care facilities (depending on type of pay-

ment plan). If you move in as a couple, when one of you dies the spouse does not have to go through the transition all alone.

2. From an economic point of view, the advantages are in the economies of scale and the access to shared resources. The amenities one shares in a CCRC go beyond what only the very wealthy could afford on their own (and even the very wealthy wouldn't want the maintenance headaches). Even in a modestly priced community, THE LAST RESORT can be like a high-end resort, often providing such expensive amenities as swimming pools, libraries, billiards rooms, maid service, greenhouses, private chapels, concierges, and a household staff. All of these services and facilities can be yours because the costs are spread over an entire community.

3. Living in a CCRC, you are likely to be part of a community of similarly-minded individuals, of similar socio-economic, intellectual, and maybe even religious background, although with diverse life experiences. While it is always possible to withdraw from the community temporarily, the dynamics of the community help to draw you back into contact with other human beings. In a CCRC you will be surrounded by people with whom and for whom to do things. Dinner conversation is often informed and stimulating— some people may have taken advantage of the time they have to think about the news, or about philosophy or religion. This is no small issue for people in the late or frail parts of life.

4. Support services are scaled to be appropriate to the age range and tastes of the residents. There are services available that you could not get outside of this kind of facility, such as

a full-time chaplain. Support facilities are appropriate—golf courses are easier to play, benches are higher so that arthritic knees don't have to bend so far to sit, walking paths are better lit, and, perhaps most important, nutrition is professionally managed to enhance well-being and health. Your house or apartment is equipped with an alarm system, and the staff people you already know are on the other end of the telephone line. In some CCRCs, residents are monitored to make sure they have not fallen and can't get up.

Simple adjustments are done proactively by professional staff, anticipating your needs. Health club facilities are inviting rather than intimidating, large print books and newspapers are available without asking, educational and recreational events are organized at a pace appropriate to people who are no longer in a hurry to get home to feed the kids and get to the PTA meeting.

5. Relationships with family and friends will not be colored by dependency. Adult daughters and sons and their spouses will not have to worry about your ability to care for yourself at home, will never have to face the relationship issues of living together with you, and will not have to make critical decisions for you. Rather, you and they will be free to enrich and deepen the relationships between yourselves as independent people and family.

In its own way, the same is also true for friends. Because you have taken responsibility for yourself in this informed and conscious choice, friendships are free to blossom. Neediness and dependency will be neither driving forces nor stumbling blocks. Relationships that might have been based on "have to" are free to become a matter of "want to."

THE CONS

1. Moving to a CCRC is a package deal. What you get is what you get. When you pay your entrance fee, you make an often irrevocable commitment to this particular CCRC with all its pluses and minuses, both now and in the future. There is no way to anticipate all that you will experience there: sales brochures are glossy and first impressions are great. Most people in most CCRCs will tell you that they love what they have and that the things that aren't perfect are only minor annoyances. However, quality of management, corporate finances, cost and techniques of care, average age and extent of thriving of residents, and availability of good help are all variables beyond your control.

2. The cost of entrance to the CCRC you want to move to may be too high either in absolute terms or because you have made decisions about where and to whom you want to leave your money when you die. Further, the projected increase in the ongoing costs may be more than you can reasonably handle.

On the other hand, if costs spiral any cap on your annual increase of fees may prevent management from maintaining the level of services you bought into. An even worse case scenario would be bankruptcy. This is an extreme case and is perhaps unlikely, but it could happen. The quality of management is critically important.

3. Because a CCRC is an entity unto itself, it is possible to find yourself disconnected from the mainstream of life. There is little exposure to children, adolescents, or young or middle-aged adults. There is equally little exposure to people in different social circumstances, except in the person of polite, self-effacing, and often low-paid staff.

4. Support services may not be state of the art. Technologies of long term health care are evolving rapidly. What is leading edge or best practices today may be obsolete well within your life expectancy. The design of a particular facility may make it impossible to stay current with best practices.

A CCRC built a decade ago may be committed to a model of care that goes from independent living directly to nursing facility without provisions for assisted living or home health care. For instance, because of commitments made in bricks and mortar, care for someone with Alzheimer's may use a hospital model rather than the more successful (but more recent) residential model. Likewise, technologies may not keep up with new practices in such areas as nutrition, exercise, activities, and education.

5. Entrance into a CCRC is a move that requires downsizing and adjustment. Family home, familiar community and congregation, long-time friends, bridge or poker buddies and volunteer groups are left behind. If there are difficulties in the lives of adult sons and daughters, there will no longer be a place for them to come home to. Grandchildren will always be very short-term visitors, and may feel pressured to be on their best behavior; they will never know the comfortable routines that their parents cherished growing up in your home. They

will never get a chance to see their grandparents on their own turf—and will not smell old family recipes being prepared in Gammie's house at Thanksgiving.

One has to make new friends, and there is a limited pool from which to draw. New friends do not have the same shared history as the old friends you left behind.

THE ISSUES

1. Entrance into a CCRC is a lifestyle choice with health-care implications rather than a health-care choice with lifestyle implications. This has important ramifications for timing. Moving to THE LAST RESORT in EXTENDED MIDDLE AGE or THE NEW ME should be something looked forward to for reasons of emotional and financial well-being. You are starting over with a new lifestyle and new friends. The sooner you make the move, the better.

The day you move in really *is* the first day of the rest of your life. The more dynamic and energetic you are, the more likely it is that you will get maximum benefit from your decision. You have not moved there to die, you have moved there to establish new, long-term relationships, to embark on a new phase of life, free of worry about eventualities. Financially, you have probably paid a significant entrance fee which may not be refundable. ENJOY! If you delay the move because you see this as a health care choice, you will have wasted the opportunity to flourish in a supportive environment.

Entrance to a CCRC depends on your ability to go into independent living and on the availability of space. People who run CCRCs and the people who live in them want you to get rooted in this lifestyle community while you are a fully functioning, capable and vitally active person. You are expected to be in EXTENDED MIDDLE AGE or THE NEW ME when you arrive. Therefore, CCRCs do not accept people whose energies are depleted because they have passed through the LIKE IT OR NOT transition. The issue is not how long you can defer moving in, but how soon you can move there.

2. Financial well-being is also an issue. Can you afford it? Let us reiterate: besides the up-front check, there are monthly fees that are tied to the cost of living. Not only must you be clear that your personal economic situation is sound, but you must make an assessment of the economic health of the CCRC and any guaranteeing institutions (such as a religious denomination). It is important for people who do not have training in finance to get professional help in making these assessments.

In CCRCs with extensive agreement payment plans, the healthy share equally in the costs of the care of the not-healthy. If the mix of those living independently and those who need care gets out of balance, either monthly fees will soar, services will be dramatically cut back, or the facility will go bankrupt.

3. Selection of which CCRC you ought to move to is a classic human dilemma. Choosing a CCRC is like choosing a college, except that instead of it being for four years (with a possible transfer of credits), this is forever. Many of the criteria are the same at a general level: where, how big, how much, what kind of people go there, do you know anybody, and can

you get in. However, you have to make this decision without the supports you had in choosing a college: family tradition, guidance counselors, *US News and World Report* rankings, published guides, and old boy/old girl networks.

Instead there are glossy marketing brochures, the occasional web site, word of mouth from friends already living there, and your own intuition. Still, a choice has to be made. These are some of the factors you will want to consider:

↪ Nearness to family and friends;

↪ Climate;

↪ Location, including local culture, shopping, faith communities, and proximity of airport or train station;

↪ Urban, suburban, or rural setting;

↪ Quality of services and presence of desired amenities, ranging from golf to chaplaincy;

↪ Age of the facility;

↪ Experience and track record of management;

↪ Access to, proximity to, and quality of acute care facilities and practitioners;

↪ Rules and regulations, such as dress codes at dinner, which can either enhance or detract from the quality of your experience.

A last and important point: CCRCs have admission requirements measured in health and financial well-being. In the case of those with payment plans based on modified or fee-for-service payment structures, adequate long term care insurance may be an entrance requirement. Another dimension of the "can you get in?" question is the length of the waiting list. We know of one CCRC where the waiting period—after acceptance and a $1,000 deposit—is nine to ten years!

4. As homey as a CCRC may be, it is an institution and one must be prepared for the investment and compromises that make living in an institution possible. Living in a CCRC requires citizenship—living out convictions about the equality and rights of all the residents, serving on committees, voting, cooperating with management, a willingness to identify problems and to care for your neighbors, particularly those whose talents and energies may not be as sharp as they once were.

THE LAST RESORT is, for some, a very attractive and accessible first choice. Properly prepared for and thoughtfully approached, it can be a fine choice. With careful planning and reflective investigation, the dream scenario can easily become a lived reality.

A THOUGHTFUL EXERCISE

In your gut, right now, do the pros of THE LAST RESORT outweigh the cons? Or, do the cons carry more weight? Try to list your strongest reactions:

1.

2.

3.

What is the most significant issue for you?

At the end of the THE FAMILY PLAN, you chose between that and HOME SWEET HOME as your choice. Do you have enough information to choose between the choice you made then and THE LAST RESORT? If so, what is your choice now?

[ ] HOME SWEET HOME [ ] THE FAMILY PLAN
[ ] THE LAST RESORT

Why?

CHAPTER SIX

The New Frontier

WHAT IT IS

THE NEW FRONTIER is the name we have given to the strategic choice to pool physical and human resources in intentional community living. The physical arrangement may take many forms, but the common core is this: people commit to each other, convinced that by drawing on the strengths and needs of the group they can do together what they could not manage on their own, and as a result they can enjoy a good old age in a non-institutional setting.

We call this THE NEW FRONTIER because it requires that people leave mainstream living arrangements and explore the uncharted terrain of life in intentional community. Examples of living arrangements for this option range from four or five people getting together to live in one house, to an eightplex shared by eight couples, to co-housing developed for 100 people by a core of people with the money and a dream. Apart from the absence of on-site health care facilities, what distinguishes THE NEW FRONTIER from THE LAST RESORT is the degree of involvement of those who live there in the formation, maintenance and management of the living situation. NEW FRONTIER developments are generally much smaller-scale than CCRCs. Those who choose THE NEW FRONTIER must make a significant commitment of personal energies to the success of the project, while professionals manage the facility for those who choose THE LAST RESORT.

THE DREAM SCENARIO

What is the dream scenario behind this strategic choice? It is very much like the commune dream of the 1960s: you find a group of people with whom you have enough in common that you can comfortably commit yourselves and your resources to each other for mutual support and care as you live from EXTENDED MIDDLE AGE through DYING. You will be self-sufficient together, where you each might have had to struggle to make it on your own.

This dream recognizes that as people age, they will have different strengths and needs. You believe that you will be able to take care of what each needs by living interdependently. You have good friends you can count on, and who can count on you. You can all continue to live securely in community way beyond the point that any of you could live alone or as a couple. You have intentionally and successfully established a way to not be alone that works for you and for your group, without moving in with your family, and without moving into an institution. Sure, it may be tough to work it out, but you can count on your resourcefulness and commitment. This is the way it should be—people were meant to live together.

THE PROS

1. Being part of an intentional, supportive community meets basic human needs that become important with increasing age. When community works, it provides psychological support, shared responsibilities and resources, a place where one does not have to carry the burdens of life by oneself, and a place where ordinary taking care is shared.

Being in community provides human resources that none but the rarest of heroes can provide individually. The need for intimacy—the need to have people to share daily life with—does not diminish with age. In the middle years the needs of intimacy are often met by couples with a wide circle of friends and acquaintances. These relationships are often grounded in work or children. With time, these circles become smaller and less sustaining. Children grow up; friends die or move away; work relationships are severed; professional and community networks get stretched thin.

People may come to the realization that their needs for sustained relationships with other people are not being met. The value of being surrounded by people who embrace life without denying death cannot be overestimated. Even life's mundane tasks can be part of personal growth if done with love.

When you live by yourself or as a couple, you have to shop, cook, clean, do repairs, do the household accounts, take out the garbage, run errands—there is stuff to do day in and day out that takes an enormous amount of time and energy at any age. All this becomes less onerous when these responsibilities are shared. Planning menus, shopping, and cooking once a week can be fun, while cooking daily is, for many, an unwelcome chore. If you only have to cook once each week, there is real and pleasurable economy of effort.

With increasing age, it becomes likely that you will have off days, no matter what phase of aging you are in. Small illnesses, chronic aches, and longer times of recuperation will diminish your ability to pull your own weight, both in tasks and in relationships. In community, ordinary taking care is shared. Neither you nor your partner have to carry the burdens of life by yourselves; you are relieved of the requirement of heroic effort. The day that your knees and ankles are killing you, you do not have to stand at the stove to cook dinner.

2. Because these are small-scale developments, arrangements for THE NEW FRONTIER are very personal. These are face-to-face, intimate, peer-nurturing groups. Because these groups are intentional, there are elements of thoughtfulness and choice in their formation that are often lacking in the happenstance of friendship. In these settings, people are brought together by common understandings of life, death, values, and religious or political sensibilities. You can expect attitudes towards sharing and selfishness that are consistent with your own. You can expect others to be open and to share a level of psychological intimacy that allows all to be not alone.

Because these communities are small, there is a level of buy-in or commitment that is unlikely in a larger context. Even in the larger formats of these types of communities (such as co-housing) where there are multigenerational possibilities, there must still be screening to ensure a basic level of compatibility.

3. Further, on account of their small scale a few people can form one of these communities on their own. You do not have to depend on some entrepreneur to raise $4 million of equity—plus the bank's money—to build a life care community where you can live. It is possible that a community such as this could be supported by a local social organization, congregation, or philanthropist.

4. There is an assumption in the formation of small-scale communities that sharing resources and space will provide economic benefits. You can't buy a tenth of a pool table, or half of a twelve-foot ladder, or a third of a swimming pool. But, one lawn service provider can mow the lawn for ten people living together at little per capita cost. If you don't like gardening but are happy as Mr. Fix-It, the human economy provides a better all-around result.

Small-scale communities may be able to afford to buy properties together at good prices. The eightplex that is deteriorating and no one wants to renovate individually might represent an excellent opportunity for a small group of couples or other family units. For some people, small communities will be the only economically feasible option short of public housing or potentially coercive family arrangements.

IS THIS A DREAM THAT RESONATES WITH YOU?

Stop a moment, and think who you might want to share with, and where you might want to establish

your own community. If you are married or already living with someone, how do you think he or she would
feel about this idea?

Who would your spouse or partner want to include?

The Cons

1. Living in community is hard work and few people are
prepared for it by training or experience. In fact, the only
experience most people have of living in community is family (as a relatively powerless child), college, or service in the
armed forces. As any honest newlywed will tell you, being part
of a group larger than one takes adjustments. Making those
adjustments at the back end of middle age or later does not
come naturally. By then you have developed patterns and ruts:
you have your own meal times and preferred foods, you do

chores more-or-less when you feel like it, and to the extent that you feel like it, and you are not used to being answerable to more than one other person.

Psychologically, community living demands honesty, sharing, loving confrontation, staying close to people over time, and surrendering to group decisions. And, to put it bluntly, there is no place in an intimate community for anyone to even flirt with another's partner. There is a very practical reason why most small, intentional communities through history have been celibate.

2. There may be people in the group who do not pull their weight even when they have no apparent excuse. There is no place in a small community for someone who is only half-heartedly part of the group. Even more critically, you are committing yourself to a group that is aging in place. Early on, it may be easy to say, "When someone gets sick we can carry them." But reality bites hard. People may be sick for a very long period of time. People may run out of resources or the ability to contribute to the group. A poignant example might be the long sorrow and debilitation of one whose life partner dies—a difficult READY OR NOT transition.

3. What happens when a group that came together in strength ages in place? How do you attract or admit new members? When a group forms, there is a bond that gives energy to the project. But how does a group attract new members when it has lived together for a number of years? Let's face it—if you were 65 or 70, would you want to join a tightly knit group of 80-year-olds who have been together for 15 years?

As a community ages in place, collective strength wanes. Earlier, there were several people in the group with strong backs. Now, there is no one without limitations. Even if the group has managed to arrange for the paid services of a helper, eventually even the energy to make decisions about repairs and maintenance may be severly diminished.

4. There are risks attached to sustaining a small community that is aging in place. Even if there are enough people at the beginning to provide a common base for nurturance, support, and sharing of chores, there are usually so few people involved that the loss of even one or two can greatly upset the balance. On a small scale, especially where you are talking about 12 or fewer people, what happens when even one can no longer take care of the activities of daily living such as bathing, dressing, eating, or controlling bowel and bladder? And then two or three of you? Here's where "Will the last one out please turn out the lights" takes on a poignancy that is hard to think about.

5. There are challenges to sustaining external relationships in a small and co-committed community. There can be a sense of exclusiveness that discourages relationships outside this group. These arrangements can sometimes breed a feeling of "us against the world." The economies of scale that are part of the strengths of these arrangements leave little physical space for adult sons and daughters, for grandchildren, or for friends from other parts of life.

6. Economic negatives may be encountered at the beginning of the project, but it is more likely that they will be

encountered later on. When a group gets together to create a community, it may underestimate the cost of the project. Even if the project manages to survive, money may need to be committed up front that will be needed later on. If reserves are consumed early, fear may undermine the project.

The economic success of such a project depends in part on the money management skills of individuals, on the general shape of the economy, and on the absence of family emergencies. People who get into an arrangement such as this under one set of economic circumstances may later find themselves in a dramatically different situation. Life is what happens when you have made other plans. Events such as an adult child getting sick or losing his or her job, significant unexpected maintenance costs, a deteriorating local economy, or reversals in the stock market can threaten the viability of the community.

If the community goes belly-up, where does the economic burden fall? It is possible that this becomes an economic meltdown that will profoundly affect the lives of all the members of the community, and all who love them.

THE ISSUES

1. Even in its smallest scale format, this is not a small-scale undertaking. If this is the strategy you choose, be prepared to plan it, build it, populate it, retrofit it, or otherwise make it happen. This is THE NEW FRONTIER. Every step along the way is either uncharted territory or, perhaps, a dimly marked trail. The chances of your efforts leading to the promised land are directly correlated to the thoroughness of your planning.

2. Consensus building, vision, and commitment to people and the project are essential elements of the planning process. It is unlikely that one charismatic person acting alone will be able to come up with a plan that enough people will buy into, although it will likely take at least one totally committed person to see the project through to the end. The process of consensus building is slow and deliberate, based on clear communications and careful thought.

Just think what people are being asked or invited to do. You and your co-adventurers are asking people to go where few have ever been. You are asking people in EXTENDED MIDDLE AGE or perhaps THE NEW ME periods of life to make bold, exciting—and frightening—choices and commitments. As the process of planning goes along, it reaches a point where commitment is essential. In a small-scale undertaking there is limited capacity to absorb people who want to get in later on, and even less for people who are in at the beginning wanting to get out.

3. There is no interpersonal contracting that means anything unless you get past the regulatory hurdles. How many unrelated people can live together in one structure? What kinds of physical facilities are you permitted to provide in this structure in this neighborhood? Most zoning codes did not contemplate these kinds of housing options, and those that did were probably designed to prevent them. In these matters, an excellent resource is *Residence Options for Older or Disabled Clients* by Lawrence A. Frolik. You will need an outstanding realtor and real estate lawyer, and Frolik's book will tell you the kinds of legal issues you will have to deal with.

4. Assuming all the hurdles are cleared, there are still the issues of interpersonal relations that need to be confronted. Issues in interpersonal relationships include (but are not limited to): a sophisticated level of skill in communications, an undying spirit of cooperation, generosity of spirit, an ability—as appropriate—to subordinate individual good to common good, and a willingness to accede to group decisions. These are not issues that can be put into legal contracts. Virtue cannot be legislated.

5. On the other hand, there are issues that do submit to and are well served by legal structures or contracts. Items such as the rights and responsibilities of mutual property ownership, the processes and procedures for admitting members to the group, the process to be implemented when a member becomes disabled or dies, exit strategies when someone wants out, inheritance, what to do when someone can no longer perform routine activities of daily living, and how liability will be shared among the group are some of the matters you will need to get agreement on and reduce to legally binding contracts.

6. Elder frailty and the inevitable limits of the community to give care will have a great impact on quality of life for the members of the community. The price of paying someone else to give that care must be taken into consideration. The group must have assurances that contingent resources will be available to pay for needed care in case it cannot be provided internally.

Before we conclude this section, we want to mention an informal version of THE NEW FRONTIER. There are small towns, tight-knit communities, residents of apartment buildings and members of congregations that undertake care of each other and those that need help without setting out any contracts or legally binding obligations. These groups take care of their own because they feel it is the right thing to do and in the expectation that, when their time comes, they will be helped in turn. We can conceive of situations in which informal versions of THE NEW FRONTIER might be made somewhat more formal without losing the character of spontaneity with which they are often blessed.

THE NEW FRONTIER is, for some of you, a very attractive choice. Properly prepared for and thoughtfully approached it can be a fine answer to the question, "Where will you live?" With careful planning and commitment, you and others of like mind and vision can turn your dream into a lived reality.

A Thoughtful Exercise
In your gut, right now, do the pros of THE NEW FRON-
TIER outweigh the cons? Or, do the cons carry more
weight? Try to list your strongest reactions:

1.

2.

3.

What is the most significant issue for you?

At the end of the The Last Resort, you chose between the first three options. Do you have enough information to choose between the choice you made then and THE NEW FRONTIER? If so, what is your choice now?

[ ] HOME SWEET HOME   [ ] THE FAMILY PLAN
[ ] THE LAST RESORT   [ ] THE NEW FRONTIER

Chapter Seven

Progressive Retreat

What It Is

Progressive Retreat means moving to the next appropriate living situation just in time. It is the strategic option to maintain your current home and lifestyle as long as desirable and then, using pre-established criteria, to move to a different place that provides the support you need. In effect, it is a strategy that uses some or all of the other options. There is an element of consciously and tenaciously holding on as long as possible to the known and familiar, but letting it go when you have to. You might hear it expressed as, "We'll deal with that when the time comes."

People who have adopted this strategy will often say things such as, "As long as we are both alive and able we will stay right here. When one of us dies or we can't manage any more, we'll move in with the kids or we'll go to the best assisted living facility we can afford. And, if it gets bad, you can put us in a nursing home." It seems perfectly reasonable and responsible. Progressive Retreat consciously tries to push back the inevitable—to push back the night—as long as possible. But it also contains a recognition that increasing levels of support are almost certainly going to be needed, an understanding of what the fall-back positions will be, and at least an implicit set of criteria for when to move on (or fall back).

The Dream Scenario

The dream scenario behind Progressive Retreat begins with a conviction that the very best place to be is right where you are. That might be the home in which you raised your family or a retirement community in Florida or Arizona (Home Sweet Home) or with one of your children (The Family Plan). The dream is that you will stay in place for a very long time—preferably forever. If it happens that you cannot manage on your own or with the help of your family and/or friends (potentially, The New Frontier), you will recognize it and move on. Grudgingly, maybe, but you will move on.

In this dream scenario, before somebody else has to move you to where you do not want to go, you will move on your own steam to a level of care and to a place you have chosen. In the dream you accept reality as it is and do what's best for everybody at each stage—but you never move into a place that offers more help than you need at that point in time. You recognize that in the end you may even need to go to a nursing home (although the majority of people do not), but you will find all sorts of ways of getting other kinds of help. And anyway, if the nursing home is absolutely the only place that can take care of you, you will deal with that when it happens but not before. After all, there is no point in borrowing worry from tomorrow.

Here is what it might look like: you stay in your own home as long as you can, and then a series of falls makes it impossible for you to bathe yourself safely or to prepare your own meals. Your children have scattered across the country, and there are no family members living in your area. All along you have thought that, when the time came, you would move into "St. Mary's Woods"—your least undesirable assisted living facility. You talk to your family and they agree that it is time for you to be somewhere where you have some help.

With only a few phone calls and a visit, you are able to find a place in St. Mary's Woods and make the arrangements to move there. Your kids all come to town and, with their help, you divvy up the stuff that you no longer need or have room for. There is remarkably little bickering—perhaps because they don't seem to treasure the same things you do. You get your house sold for more money than you can remember having in one check in all your life, and those nagging worries about outliving your assets are relieved.

The days at St. Mary's Woods are pleasant enough. At first, you play cards almost every day, and even make a few new friends. Your children call every week just after you move in, but then less and less often. After a few years you become so frail that even getting out of bed or sitting in a chair at the dining room table without assistance is beyond you. It has been a long time since you took a bath or shower by yourself. Reluctantly, you concede that you must move to the "Christopher

Home"—the best nursing care facility in the city. Despite a couple of bouts in the hospital, you are able to wait until a room becomes available. The people at St. Mary's Wood help you to make the arrangements and you are moved.

Relieved of almost all the demands of everyday living by the appropriate supportive services, you make a few new acquaintances and pass your days in satisfying fashion. Your children come to visit occasionally, you stay warm and dry and are fed decent food, and you live there, relatively comfortably, until you die in your sleep after a few months.

The Pros

1. Where you live is home. It is familiar and comfortable. It is adequate and there is no reason to leave it. It is "Home Sweet Home."

2. Staying where you are means that perhaps there will never be a need to move at all—or to decide what to keep and what to throw away, and who gets what, or to ride the emotional roller-coaster of sorting through years of memories.

3. From an economic point of view, this could be a low-cost option, especially if you don't have a long REST OF LIVING period. You already own the house and may even have paid off the mortgage. If you rent, you may be protected by law from large rent increases. You get to defer (and maybe even avoid) the cost of moving.

4. If you have not already taken the strategic option of moving in with your children (THE FAMILY PLAN), in PROGRESSIVE RETREAT you won't move in with them too early.

You will avoid being with them longer than necessary. When the time comes, what are perceived as relatively short-term arrangements may be tailored to meet everyone's needs. And besides, it may make sense for one of the grandchildren to move in with you. As the lyricist said, "With a little bit of luck, they'll grow up and start supporting you!"

5. Technology may make a move unnecessary. Technology includes systems of support and monitoring, community resources, community involvement, and health care delivery. Aging is a dynamically developing field. Ten years ago there was no such thing as assisted living. It is likely that technologies of support or care might be available ten years from now that are not even on the drawing boards today.

THE CONS

1. Even if the house itself does not become a functional or safety problem, home is not a static reality. It includes a network of relationships that will inevitably dwindle as years pass and other people move or die. Home is a fragile human and relational construct that is often confused with bricks and mortar construction. There may come a time when the neighborhood changes so dramatically that you want to leave but, because you chose to wait, you can no longer find any place to go or any way to get there.

2. A sudden decline in health—a crippling stroke, for example—may preclude your planned next choice. You may find yourself unable to qualify for admission to a CCRC, in need of too much care for assisted living, and too healthy and independent-minded to move to a nursing home. When

Henry's mother became too frail to continue to live on her own, she moved to a fine assisted living facility in her town. It had opened just weeks before she absolutely had to move .Her alternative was a nursing home 130 miles away. The assisted living facility could just as easily have opened a month too late, or filled up a week too soon, and you can't plan to be that lucky.

3. The longer you defer the move, the more difficult it will be. This strategic option presumes "just in time" moving, which by definition means less strength and stamina, fewer physical and mental resources, and more persistent emotional stress. Under the best of circumstances, moving is hard. A move deferred until there is no choice is the hardest of all.

4. Economically, deferring a move may be very costly. You may not be able to get access to where you want to go, or demand may have pushed prices up above what you can afford. The cost of retrofitting your house so that you can stay there may have passed a break-even point.

5. Your family and interpersonal realities and dynamics change. What is now a stable situation for an adult son or daughter, spouse, and family may change so that what is possible now may not be possible when you decide it is time to move in with them. Nobody is wrong, they just live in a different world. Even if people have agreed to have you move in "when the time comes," they did so based on what they understood that to mean then. For a world of good reasons, when the time comes they may no longer be willing or able to accommodate you.

6. While technology may develop more and better options in the delivery of services, it may also close off options or force you to use technologies with which you are uncomfortable. Implicit in any improved delivery of services is an economy of scale which may or may not include single family dwellings, may or may not include your neighborhood, and may or may not include the managed care plan of which you are a member. Your projections of how home services technology will better serve you in the future may not turn out to be the case at all.

Changes in Medicare, Medicaid, Social Security and insurance programs may also work to either force or facilitate your PROGRESSIVE RETREAT. These are all part of the technology of aging support in the future, but may not develop in just the way you are counting on them to.

THE ISSUES

1. Can you pull it off? Will you really follow through and do it? Can you defeat Cleopatra—the Queen of Denial—and really make it happen?

2. To be successful, PROGRESSIVE RETREAT requires very, very good timing. This choice has at its core that you will only retreat at the optimum moment. What is a stake, then, is whether, at the optimum moment, all the resources required will be available. You will recognize it as the time to go and be able to find a desirable place into which to move, the financial resources to move there, and the physical, emotional, and relational resources to do the move and start over satisfacto-

rily in a new place even though your personal strengths are diminished.

As a practical matter, timing is such an issue that it could defeat the strategy.

3. Beyond the issue of timing, PROGRESSIVE RETREAT requires sustained good judgement about what is really best in any given "here and now." When you are hale and hearty, you can build a plan founded on a commitment to make your moves before the financial, emotional, and human costs to you and others become too great. It is difficult to recognize and act on those costs when you are in the midst of them, and to have the courage to implement your plan.

This strategic option has explicit dimensions (plans) and implicit dimensions (tangles of hopes, values and assumptions) that may not even be known until you actually try to work them out. When you live in the midst of gradual and almost imperceptible diminishment, you make daily adjustments that you hardly notice. Your world may appear safer and more stable than it really is. Thus, you may come to the point where you are unwilling to make a move, even though you have reached the point where, in better times, you yourself said you would do so. To be successful, this strategic option needs at least yearly review.

4. There is an economic issue that is like "the fallacy of the beard." In medieval logic, there was a fallacy by that name in which a person claimed to be able to prove that a beard was made up of only one hair. The argument went like this: show me a person whom we both agree has a beard. Then let me

pull out one hair at a time. After pulling out each hair, I ask whether or not this person still has a beard. At some point after I pull out just one more hair you have to say, "No, now he no longer has a beard." "See," I then say, "one hair does make a beard."

The economic considerations in PROGRESSIVE RETREAT resemble this fallacy. While we cannot say at what precise point it gets to be economically unwise to stay in one's own home, at some point the person who chooses PROGRESSIVE RETREAT beginning with HOME SWEET HOME may cross this line. The crossover point might have to do with deferred maintenance, with decline in property values, with cessation of equity build-up, or with the cost of maintaining a home for one person that barely made sense for two people. There are many straws that could break this camel's back.

5) Every strategic option requires attention to others as well as to yourself. There are no exceptions. Although PROGRESSIVE RETREAT is not necessarily a selfish strategic choice, it carries with it the danger of making decisions without adequate regard to the impact on those who have to bear the weight of your decisions. It is one thing to have a mutually agreed-upon plan about when and under what circumstances you will make a move; it is another, given human fallibility, to carry it through.

In no way, however, do we discount PROGRESSIVE RETREAT as a viable strategy. You and we both know of instances where it has worked beautifully. PROGRESSIVE RETREAT is, for some of you, a sensible and attractive choice. Approached thoughtfully and with maturity, it can be a best choice. With a balance between not borrowing worry from tomorrow and commitment to facing the truth, you can turn this dream scenario into a reality.

So, what choice do you or you and your spouse or partner make? Will you stay in the house you call home until they carry you out in a pine box? Or, will you move in with one of your children? Is it time to start looking at CCRCs? Or will you get together with Bob and Sally and Jan and Pete to talk about buying a piece of land to build a nice, small community? Or, will you just stay where you are until you have to move on?

Whatever you decide, now you have got a clearer picture of what your choices are, and what you need to consider. Home is where the heart is, and that is surely part of the practical foundation for thriving.

A THOUGHTFUL CONCLUSION
(At least, a tentative conclusion.)

Some of you are in a place right now where you can say, "This is MY answer to the question of where I will live while I age." Are you one of those? If so, what is your choice?

[ ] HOME SWEET HOME [ ] THE FAMILY PLAN
[ ] THE LAST RESORT [ ] THE NEW FRONTIER
[ ] PROGRESSIVE RETREAT

Congratulations!

Now, is there anything you have to do to make it happen? If so, what?

If you need more information to make a decision, what information do you need?

If the problem is that you and your spouse or partner can't agree, what steps will you take to reach a mutually acceptable choice?

A Postscript to SECTION TWO

We have not mentioned suicide as a solution to frailty. This omission is deliberate. We recognize that some people of great integrity will, in extreme circumstances, make the moral choice to end life by either active or passive means. We make no judgement about their decisions except to note that many could go on living and thriving were better care and supportive services more widely available.

We recognize that some others may dismiss the hard issues of planning for frailty with a cavalier "If it comes to that, I'll shoot myself!" That is not planning; it is denial. It has nothing to do with planning to thrive for the whole of one's life, or to fully live the rest of your life.

How Will You Pay for It?

In Section Two you dealt with "Where will you live?"—the first strategic question for establishing a practical foundation for fully living the rest of your life. This section is about the second strategic question: "How will you pay for it?" It, in this case, is the financial expense associated with the phases and stages of the rest of your life.

The thing about living in America is that it takes money. That is not to say that the more money you have the more you thrive. We know some very wealthy people who are very unhappy. And, like us, you probably know many people whose income and wealth are decidedly modest but who are nonetheless very happy, and are living their lives fully. It does not take a great deal of wealth to support thriving at any age and, clearly, money does not buy happiness.

At the same time, even a modest lifestyle needs some income behind it, and we assume that if you are reading this book you have an expectation of a certain lifestyle that you want to maintain from EXTENDED MIDDLE AGE right through the DYING transition. We also assume you have some idea of what that will cost, at least as measured in today's dollars. Two aspects of aging make paying attention to money especially important:

⟿ It is the only part of life other than childhood in which people plan not to work to earn an income; and

⟿ It is a stage of life where at some point most people can expect to have $3,500 or more—maybe much more—added to their monthly budget for frailty care.

The good news is that we are all living longer. The bad news is that nobody told your money.

Making sure that your economic concerns have been anticipated and prepared for is part of fully living the rest of your life. A sense of economic security, along with an informed choice about where you will live through all the stages and phases of aging, taken together, create a practical foundation for thriving.

QUESTIONS AND STEPS

There is a fundamental question for this section, then, which is "How do you provide for financial security throughout aging?" That question is like a three-legged stool, and all three legs must be in place to provide stability. Think of the three legs as three more specific questions. Those questions are:

1. *If you stop working, what will you live on?* If you want to stop working for a living at some point in EXTENDED MIDDLE AGE or beyond, or if you get to the point where you must stop

working because of a physical or cognitive limitation or some legal requirement, what financial resources will you have available to support your lifestyle? There are only three possible sources of income: people at work, money at work, or benefit plans, which are a combination of the first two. Answering the "If you stop working, what will you live on?" question is what retirement income planning is normally about.

2. *How will you pay for frailty care?* If you or your spouse or partner becomes frail, how will you pay for the medical and supportive care that you will need, especially if (when) you lose your ability to function independently? Although there are regional variations, the price of frailty care is somewhere around $4,000 per month, and it can be more than twice that in some big cities like New York or Boston. Answering the "How will you pay for frailty care?" question is what frailty planning is normally about.

3. *What will happen to what you have, and to anyone who depends on what you have, when you die?* Who is economically dependent on you, and how do your assets need to be arranged to take care of them when you die? How will your estate be administered and distributed, and how much of it will be lost to taxes? How will assets with ongoing existences that affect other people, such as family businesses, be dealt with? Answering the "What will happen to what you have when you die?"question is what estate planning is normally about.

Answering these three questions constitutes the process of providing for financial security throughout aging. And, while the emphasis and focus of answering each of these questions differs, three steps take place in the process of answering each of them:

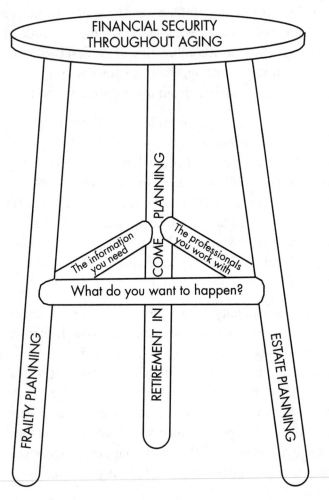

a. *What do you want to happen?* The first step in answering each of these three questions is to determine the desired outcome. In retirement income planning, this has to

do with determining how much income needs to be generated, how it will be generated, and when it will start and how
long it has to last. In frailty planning, this step has to do with
determining where you want to receive care and how you will
pay someone to provide it. In estate planning, this has to do
with determining what people and institutions you want to
provide for, and whether you have any assets that need special
consideration or attention.

b. *What information do you need?* The next step is to
gather the information you need to find out where you are
now. Although others can try to do this for you, it is a task best
done by you. You have the relationships where you work to get
benefit information, you are the policyholder calling the
insurance company for information, and so on. Because of
heightened sensitivity to privacy issues, even formal letters of
authorization may not be enough for someone else to do this
groundwork for you.

c. *What do you do to get the outcome you want?* The
final step is to develop a plan to get you from where you are to
where you want to be, and to implement it. This step normally
requires professional help.

In the next chapters you will be prompted to develop your
thinking about what you want to have happen in the areas of
retirement income, frailty, and estate planning, and you will
be guided in gathering the information you need to determine where you are now. In the cases of retirement income
and estate planning, this is primarily information about you.
In the case of frailty planning, this is primarily information
about options that are available that you need to be aware of.

Lastly, you will learn how to identify a good person or good people to work with in areas where you need professional help. At the end of this section, you will be well on your way to financial security throughout aging.

How Much Does Frailty Care Really Cost?

Late in 1999 we called more than two dozen highly skilled Geriatric Case Managers around the country to find out how much frailty care really costs. These are some of the people we spoke with. They are all members of the National Association of Professional Geriatric Care Managers (1604 North Country Club Road, Tucson, AZ 86716; phone: (520)-881-8008) and some of them serve or have served as officers of the Association.

Rona Bartlestone, MSW, LCSW, BCD
  Rona Bartlestone Associates. Inc., Ft. Lauderdale, FL
Steven Barlam, MSW, LCSW
  Senior Care Management, Beverly Hills, CA
Marian Bruin, MSW, ACSW, BCD
  Star Systems Consultation and Training, Tampa, FL
Meredith Patterson, MSW, LICSW, CMC
  Meredith Patterson Associates, Concord, MA

Mary M. Miner, MSN. RN
    Miner and Associates, Ellicott City, MD
Nancy Alterman, LCSW
    Vorhees, NJ
Eleanor Rubin, MA, BA
    Eleanor S. Rubin Associates, Wachtung, NJ
Claudia Fine, MSW, MPH
    Fine and Newcombe Associates, New York, NY
Juanita Nealer, ACSW, LSW
    Pittsburgh, PA
Marion Thompson, MS
    Intervention Associates, Inc., Wayne, PA
Marianne Ewig, MSW, ACSW, BS
    September Managed Care, Milwaukee, WI

We asked them to tell us the range of costs in their area for a Nurse's Aide or Home Health Aide, a non-Medicare nursing or other skilled professional visit, a 24-hour live-in, a semi-private room in a nursing home, and care coordination. We asked them how competitive those costs were in their area. They shared their fees with us on the condition that we not publish them in such a way that what they charged could be linked directly to them (which seemed reasonable enough).

Here is what they told us: The cost of a Nurse's Aide or Home Health Aide ranged from a low of about $9/hour for a contract worker (i.e. a worker who is not a direct employee and recieves no benefits) to a high of $30/hour. The average rate sorted out at about $15/hour. Thus, for an 8-hour shift the cost to you is about $120.

For around-the-clock care at your home (24 hours, in a situation where the worker can get a full night's sleep) the cost runs between $135 and $200 per day. This multiplies out to between $49,275 and $73,000 per year. The high end of the range in some areas soared to over $300 per day—over $100,000 per year.

Until October of 1998, visits by nurses and other skilled professionals (Occupational Therapists, Speech Therapists, Physical Therapists) have usually been covered by Medicare. However, if they are not, the average visit runs about $70—with wide variations.

Care coordinators cost between $85 and $150 per hour. That is money you cannot afford to save. (And they did not ask us to say that!)

Nursing home costs run between $130 and well over $200 per day, some over $300 per day. That multiplies out to a range from $47,450 to $73,000 per year, and over $100,000 at the high end. We are not aware of any facilities anywhere for less than $95 per day.

CHAPTER EIGHT

Beginning the Process

Retirement income planning, frailty planning, and estate planning all involve complex issues and sophisticated tools and techniques. The three planning processes have grown up in different business communities: retirement income planning in the securities brokerage and mutual fund communities, frailty planning in the legal and health care communities, and estate planning in the legal and life insurance communities.

But the planning processes need to interact with each other. To plan for the financial aspects of aging without considering all three is to build your financial future on a one- or two-legged stool. Neither is stable. Planning to accumulate wealth to replace the money you earn when you work with so-called "unearned income," without also considering your possible need for resources for frailty care, is worse than an unfortunate oversight. Frailty planning that depends on spending assets to provide needed supportive and health care services without taking into account the impact of such a plan on income or reserves takes much too narrow a focus. Taking great pains to structure an estate plan to minimize taxation without also considering a survivor's needs for income and frailty care is an incomplete and inadequate effort. And so on.

TIMING

Notice that the terms retirement income planning, frailty planning, and estate planning each end with the same word. Each has the word "planning" in its title. That is not a coincidence. It is never too soon to plan for retirement income, or to plan for frailty, or to plan your estate, but it can be too late.

In the case of retirement income planning, if you really decide that retiring from working is something you want to do at age 61, you are much more likely to be able to save and invest enough money to make that possible if you start at age 40 than if you start at age 57. That is not to say that there is nothing that can be done if you have already lived six decades, haven't put anything aside, and just can't stand your job any more, but in those circumstances your options are much more limited. Much of the foundation of retirement income planning is the effect of compound interest, which has only two variables: time and rate. The more time you give yourself (the sooner you start), the less risk you will have to undertake to get the rate you need. Converesely, the longer you wait to start planning for money at work to replace you at work, the more you will be at the mercy of long-shot investments.

You may think that frailty planning differs from retirement income or estate planning—that it cannot be done until you are frail. That is not the case. While a specific care plan can only be developed in response to your needs when you can no longer function independently, the setting in which you receive care and the kind of care you get can be anticipated and planned for. Your answer to the question, "Where will you live?" includes the core of your frailty care plan, but it will only be useful if it has been implemented before the LIKE IT OR NOT transition occurs. In frailty planning this is the cardinal rule: "Better five years too soon than five minutes too late."

Even with the best of intentions and rock-solid family relationships, adult daughters and sons may not be physically close enough to do in-person caregiving at the time when you need it. The number of Baby Boomers providing long-distance care is expected to double over the next fifteen years, according to a study by the National Council on the Aging (NCOA) and the Pew Charitable Trusts. The specifics of these arrangements are not forseeable in detail today. But we know that without frailty planning, the details of these situations will be much less satisfactory for all concerned than they could have been and would have been with frailty planning.

By definition, estate planning must be done in advance. There can be no planning for estate distribution after you have died. If you haven't made provisions for what is to go to whom, the state or commonwealth in which you live has. It is never too soon to write your will or have it written. Similarly, if someone is dependent on your estate for an income on which to live, you need to plan for that while you are alive (and maybe while you are still insurable) because after you die is just too late.

The Question Only You Can Answer: What Do you Want to Happen?

No one else can articulate your dreams and desires. Your first step—and no one can do it but you—is to determine where you want each of these planning processes to lead (see illustration, page 112.).

Retirement Income Planning

What does "retirement" mean to you? Do you spell retirement G-O-L-F? Or T-R-A-V-E-L? Do you really want to retire, or do you just want to do something different? Is fifteen or twenty or more years of vacation all that inviting, or is redirection what you are trying to accomplish? Do you just want to slow down a little?

Perhaps you really want to quit what you have been doing since you were in your late twenties and take off six months or a year or even two, then maybe go back to school. Perhaps there is a hobby you want to turn into a profession, or a passion you want to perfect. Perhaps you want to take up a lower-paid profession or engage wholeheartedly in some volunteer work. Do you want to take your retirement in installments, two or three years at a time bracketing decades of working? Does the notion of retirement even apply to you?

Everybody has a personal dream about what it means to retire, or at least to live the last third of their life, and there is no point trying to generalize it. The only dream that matters is yours. What is it? What do you want to do for the rest of your life? What is it that will most delight *you* and is most likely to support *your* thriving?

As you think about the period from EXTENDED MIDDLE AGE through DYING, how would you like to spend the time of your life? Really, deep down in your heart?

How do you think your spouse or partner would like to spend it?

Now, you two really should talk about this!

Given that you have some initial ideas about what you want to do, how much income will you need, and where will it come from? There are three scenarios. In the first, you quit working altogether; in the second, you work part-time for a certain length of time or off-and-on; in the third, you embark on a project that has start-up costs and potential income.

If you quit working altogether, you need to ask this question: "What percentage of the income you are living on now, or what amount of money, will you need to maintain the lifestyle you want?" The answer to this question is sometimes called the replacement ratio. You can use a widely accepted rule of thumb: you will need 75% of your pre-retirement gross income to retire at the same standard of living. Alternatively, you can develop a more detailed budgeting approach. In either case, beware of false precision. Absolute accuracy is not necessary. Round your needs up and your resources down to stay on the safe side.

If you choose to take the more detailed approach, start with your gross income. If you are making $60,000 a year now, you won't need $60,000 a year to retire at the same standard of living because there are costs associated with working that will disappear or be significantly reduced when you retire. You will have to subtract all of those expenses (such as Social Security taxes, contributions to 401(k) or other savings plans at work, and non-work-related savings) from your income, because you live on what you keep, not what you make. Theoretically, at least, what you have been saving for is at hand, so there is no longer as strong a need to save for the future. You have not been spending your whole gross income, but rather some smaller amount, while setting aside money for retirement and emergencies. It is that smaller number that you have been living on that you need to focus on.

You then have to add in any additional expenses that you will incur after you retire. If your dream has been to retire to play golf every day, your green fees will be higher after you retire than they were when you were working five days a week. If, however, you choose to volunteer your time and expertise to some worthy cause, it is likely that you will incur little or no expense in doing so.

Life is a long journey, and getting longer. Living on money at work and benefit plans for a third of your life can certainly be done—with some amount of luck, good planning, and a stock market that keeps going up—but only you can decide if you will thrive doing so.

If you work part-time, you need to ask this question: "How much money can you count on making after quitting your career job, and for how long?" You may dream about slowing down and getting rid of some of the stress, but not quitting work completely. Circumstances change, so only plan on this income for a year or two at a time. What you choose to do to be fully alive may develop as you actually experience this way of life.

If you embark on a project with start-up costs and potential income, the question you need to ask is this: "How much money will you need for start-up and operating costs, and when will you likely turn a profit, and of how much?" Perhaps your dream has been to establish a Bed and Breakfast on the coast of Maine. You will need enough money to make at least a down payment, and to do whatever restoration is required, and to fund a marketing budget, and to pay the bills until the guests start arriving—and to have a reserve in case they don't come as quickly as you had hoped.

In each of the scenarios, the questions you need to ask are intimately tied to what you want to do. How much income the retirement planning process has to provide for is tied to what you want to do with the last third of your life.

Don't try to factor in inflation at this point. Let the professionals you work with do that with you. The reason is that there are a number of approaches that can be taken, and whichever one you use must be used consistently in all calculations. You cannot pick an inflation assumption without simultaneously picking an investment yield assumption. In other words, it is possible to both confuse and concern yourself unnecessarily. If you will do the work that only you can do—deciding what your desired end result is—you will have made a major contribution to a successful effort with your planning partner. Inflation needs to be accounted for, but not without guidance and not at this stage.

FRAILTY PLANNING

The bulk of what you want to happen in terms of frailty care is tied to your choice of where to live in aging. For instance, if you choose HOME SWEET HOME, you have also chosen home care should you (or your spouse or partner) pass through the LIKE IT OR NOT transition into dependence. Similarly, should you choose THE FAMILY PLAN or THE NEW FRONTIER, you have chosen to be cared for at your adopted home, unless there is some element of PROGRESSIVE RETREAT built into your living arrangements by prior agreement. If you choose THE LAST RESORT, with an extensive agreement payment plan, there is no question that you have done the core of your frailty planning! You might want to revisit the "Where will you live?" question at this point, or this may serve to confirm the decision you have made. In either event, if you are married or living with a partner, be sure to consider what will happen when one of you is left alone.

This is also a good time to talk through your feelings and desires with regard to such things as Do Not Resuscitate (DNR) orders, organ donation, and medical heroics. Resolving these matters is no less important than having a will, and may affect you a great deal more.

A sophisticated approach to frailty care distinguishes between caregiving and loving. What role do you want family and friends to perform for you?

What do you want to be able to hire someone to do?

How about your spouse or partner?

ESTATE PLANNING

The estate planning questions have to do with beneficiaries and assets. The first is, "Who are the people or institutions or organizations that you want to provide for after you have died?" Who those beneficiaries are is generally pretty straightforward: in terms of people, it is usually your spouse or partner, or your children or grandchildren, or maybe nieces or nephews or special friends. Some of them will be people you feel compelled to provide for—people who are dependent on your money to support their living. Others will be people or institutions or organizations you would like to provide for, out of love or gratitude. Perhaps you feel that way about your church, or a charity that has meant a lot to you during your lifetime, or your college.

"How do you want to provide for these beneficiaries?" is another question. You might want to leave a lump sum of money, or a stream of income, or a combination of the two. How much do you want to assure each of them has after you die? Is it important that all your beneficiaries receive equal value? If not, how will you determine who gets how much? This is one of the few areas of life where "because I said so" is all the reason you need—provided you are working out of your best and truest self.

A related issue has to do with anything you own that has special significance outside of its value, such as a family heirloom or a piece of art. What do you want to be sure happens to these things? Who do you want to get them? How will you maintain equity among all the recipients of your estate? You might want to consider making a game of "who gets what." We know one family where the matriarch called her two daughters and her son and his wife together, dumped all her very fine jewelry on the table, and declared: "Now, let's see you all sort out who gets what!" Distributing the family jewels may not be your specific problem, and this style of interaction may not be one you are comforatble with, but you get the idea.

Major assets with lives of their own, such as a family business, pose other issues that go far beyond the scope of this book. Planning for how to deal with these kinds of assets is critical, but absolutely should not be undertaken without professional help.

Are there people you *need* to provide for after you die, anyone who is completely—or in large part— dependent on your money to support their living?

1.

2.

Who would you *like* to provide for?

1.

2.

How do you want to provide for your beneficiaries? Do they need income, or assets, or both? How much?

1.

2.

What assets do you have that need special attention?

1.

2.

3.

4.

Who should get them? How will you determine that?

1.

2.

3.

4.

∝

FINDING A PLANNING PROFESSIONAL

After you have done what only you can do, there is a great deal of expertise needed to help you structure and implement your plan. That is a job for a professional. You may find such a person in any of a number of disciplines, and they go by a variety of titles. You might work with an insurance agent, a stockbroker, a financial planner, a lawyer or an accountant. She or he may be called a Retirement Planning Consultant or an Estate Planner or an Elder Law Attorney—or something altogether different.

There are many designations that are an indication of some expertise in the financial dynamics of aging. CFP, CLU, ChFC, CPA, and LLB or JD are examples. Some of the very best practitioners have no initials after their names. An important consideration is how well the person understands the human dynamics of aging, as well as the financial dynamics. Money evokes strong emotional reactions, and planning for financial security throughout aging must account for both the emotional and financial impacts of using various tools and techniques.

Planners who maintain membership in the National Council on the Aging (NCOA), or the American Society on Aging (ASA), or The National Institute on Financial Issues and Services for Elders (NIFSE) or other aging organizations may be more likely to have this orientation, but such membership is not really a credential. Nor is there any professional certification that indicates competence in integrating all the financial dynamics of aging with the human dynamics. No doubt, new certifications will be created as Baby Boomers turn more and more attention to this process and demand a comprehensive, coordinated approach to putting a practical foundation under fully living the rest of your life.

There is no simple test that will assure that you are dealing with a competent and honest practitioner, so don't be afraid to interview several. You should not incur any expense for these exploratory visits other than your time. Find someone you feel comfortable with, who you think will deal with you fairly and who is up front about both how he or she gets paid and the areas in which she or he has expertise. Find out if they understand aging, and are active in the community of aging professionals. Find out if they are comfortable saying "I don't know, but I can find out," or "I don't handle that, but I have a working relationship with someone who does."

It is unreasonable to expect one person to have great expertise in all areas, and in some cases legal and ethical issues prevent practitioners from crossing boundaries. It is also unreasonable of a practitioner to think that he or she has expertise in all areas; be wary of any who tell you they do. On the other hand, you do want to work with someone who is aware of all the issues that must be dealt with. There is a distinction between not being an expert and not knowing enough to ask about or to consider all the issues at stake.

Nor does any industry have a corner on expertise, although some, such as the legal community, have the exclusive right to do some of what needs to be done. You will need to ascertain what people can and cannot do legally; they will know. Do not be afraid to ask them. The financial security to fully live the rest of your life is at stake.

When you interview people, ask about fees and fee structures, and whether they get commissions on anything they might recommend. It will help if you determine in advance how you feel about people only getting paid by commissions and whether you would rather pay a fee to prevent conflicts of interest (if their licensing permits).

If you are talking to an insurance agent, you will want to know whether he or she is a "career agent" with one company. A career agent hasn't spent his or her entire career with one company; rather one company provides a career agent's training, office space or allowance, and administrative support—in exchange for a first call on their business. Career agents often have access to other companies' products, but do not underestimate the pressure these agents are under to make sales for their primary company. On the other hand, career agents have direct access to a lot of information and professional support from their primary company that might be provided to you either very inexpensively or free of charge. If the primary company does not have a certain line of products, it may be a problem because you may never be told about exactly what you need!

Regardless of the professional background and affiliations of the people you interview, you should ask for references, and to see samples of their work. Ask if they regularly review clients' situations, and what their methodology is for doing so. Are you comfortable that you will not be forgotten?

You should probably start looking for someone to work with soon after you have begun thinking about what you want to happen in the way of retirement income planning, frailty planning, and estate planning. If you wind up dealing with a different person or firm for each area, who will make sure that all the plans interact appropriately? Is that a task you are comfortable taking on? Only you can determine what you are trying to accomplish in retirement income planning, frailty planning, and estate planning, and only you can choose a planning partner or partners.

CHAPTER NINE

The Information You Need

The next step in the process is a set of tasks that others can do for you, but you can best do for yourself: collecting the data you need in order to do the planning. Gathering the facts of your situation is time-consuming and can often be confronting, but it must be done. Given that it is true that "If you don't know where you are going, any road will take you there," it is equally true that if you don't know your starting point, you will get lost on any path. What follows are questions you need to answer to establish your starting points for retirement income planning, estate planning and frailty planning—the financial dynamics of aging.

RETIREMENT INCOME PLANNING

1. Are you, or is your spouse, fully qualified for Social Security retirement benefits? Credits determine whether or

not you are *qualified* for Social Security, but your Social Security *benefit* is a percentage of your earnings averaged over most of your working lifetime. In 1999, you received one Social Security credit for each $740 of earnings, up to the maximum of four credits per year. The projected amount for a credit in 2000 is $780. Before 1999 you didn't have to earn as much income—$700 in 1998, for example—to earn a Social Security credit. In future years, the amount of earnings needed for a credit will rise as average earnings levels rise. Everyone born in 1929 or later needs 40 credits to be eligible for Social Security retirement benefits.

If you were born in 1937 or earlier, you can receive your full retirement benefit at age 65. If you were born in 1960 or later, you cannot receive your full retirement benefit until age 67. If you were born between 1938 and 1959, you qualify for full retirement benefits somewhere between age 65 and age 67, according to the following chart:

1938	65 and 2 months	1955	66 and 2 months
1939	65 and 4 months	1956	66 and 4 months
1940	65 and 6 months	1957	66 and 6 months
1941	65 and 8 months	1958	66 and 8 months
1942	65 and 10 months	1959	66 and 10 months
1943-1954	66	1960	67

Late in 1999, the Social Security Administration began mailing Social Security Statements each year to all workers age 25 and older who are not already receiving monthly Social Security benefits. You should get yours approximately 3 months before your birthday. If you have not, or would like a more current estimate of the retirement, disability and survivors' benefits that would be payable to you and your family, call Social Security at 1-800-772-1213 and follow their automated voice system. Or, you can request an estimate over the internet at http://www.ssa.gov. Just click on the Social Security Statement graphic on their home page. Their system will walk you through either making the request online (the information will be sent to you in the mail) or printing out the form that you can fill out and mail in to get the information.

2. Do you have a pension plan, or pension plans? This does not mean an IRA or a profit sharing plan or a 401(k) or 403(b) (often known as a tax-sheltered annuity, or TSA, and mostly for teachers and ministers and employees of not-for-profits); those are really tax-advantaged savings plans from which you will most likely get a lump sum of money. They will be covered next. You will probably only be able to get a monthly income from a pension plan, rather than a lump sum benefit. If you have one, another set of questions needs answers:

a. How much income will you receive from your pension plan, starting when? Do you have choices about when to start getting income, or does it automatically start at some point (for example, the 1st day of the month following your 65th birthday)?

b. If you have choices, how does the benefit change if you start receiving it before your normal retirement date? How does it change if you keep working until some later date?

c. Does the amount of your pension change with inflation every year?

You can get the answers to these questions from the Human Resources or Employee Benefits Department, or whoever administers the benefit plans where you work. Don't forget places where you have worked in the past and have vested benefits. Ask for the answers in writing (because you will need to take them with you when you go to see a professional), and if you do not understand the answers you get, speak with the plan administrator. It is likely that it will be easy to get a comfortable understanding of what you have and a projection of what benefits you will have at normal retirement age and at other optional retirement ages.

3. What other plans do you have from work? Do you have a 401(k) plan or a 403(b) plan? Do you have a SEP (Simplified Employee Benefit) plan, or an HR-10 plan (sometimes called a Keogh Plan)? Do you have any deferred compensation plans, or any other retirement-related benefits from work?

What you will need to know about these plans is how much they are worth today and how much they will be worth at various projected dates or ages. The professional you work with will help you to forecast future values, but the plan administrator should be able to give you a standard benefit projection. How much you have been putting into them, and how much you think you will continue to put into them for how long, are pieces of information you will need to supply. You will also need to know whether any of them have any income options included (can you get the benefit as a stream of income?), or whether they are all just pots of money.

4. What are your personal financial assets?

    a.   What are your banking assets? What are the average balances in your checking and savings accounts? How are those accounts titled? Are they in your name, your spouse's or partner's name, or joint title? Or are they held in joint title with a sibling or child, or under a Uniform Gifts to Minors custodianship? Do you have any CDs? When do they expire?

    b.   Do you have an IRA, either Roth or regular, or do you and your wife or partner have more than one? Who is the owner, and who is the beneficiary? What is the value today, how much are you putting in every year, and how long do you plan to keep putting money in?

    c.   Do you have any stocks, bonds, or mutual funds? Whose name are they in? You will need to know their current market value and how much you paid for them. It will also be helpful to your planning partner if you can articulate why you own what you own—what your investment criteria are.

    d.   Do you or your spouse or partner have any Managed Accounts, sometimes known as wrap accounts? Who is managing the money? How often do you have an opportunity to review performance? How much are you paying in fees?

    e.   Do you or your spouse or partner have any annuities, either fixed, variable, or equity-indexed? What is their annuitization value, and their surrender value? How liquid are they (what charges will be imposed if you surrender them or try to convert the asset to a stream of income)? Do any of them have conditional increased benefits payable if you cannot perform certain activities of daily living or suffer a cognitive impairment?

f.   Do you have any life insurance cash values? Are your policies traditional whole life, universal life, variable life, or equity indexed? If you have traditional whole life policies, what dividend option are you using to manage them? Do any of your life insurance policies have any conditional benefits for long term care?

5. Do you anticipate any inheritances? Approximately how much do you expect to inherit? Under what circumstances (who has to die)? When might those circumstances come to pass (how old is he or she, how healthy—and how committed to living a long life)?

6. What real estate do you own? What is the approximate value of your home? When you first took out your mortgage, how much did you borrow, at what interest rate, and for how many years? Do you have a second mortgage, or other debts secured by the house?

Do you own any rental property or raw land? Did you borrow money to acquire any of these assets? On what terms?

7. What other debts do you have? Credit card balances? Personal loans? Margin account balances?

8. Are there any other financial facts in your situation, such as alimony or estate distribution requirements to a former spouse? Anything else that impacts you?

ESTATE PLANNING

Generally, the information you need for estate planning is the same information you gathered for retirement income planning, except in two areas.

1. If you or your spouse has a pension plan, does the plan pay benefits for as long as the retired worker lives, or do you have choices about what kind of guarantees you can have? For instance, can you take the pension benefit so that it will pay the same amount for as long as you live and as long as your spouse lives? If you choose that option, how much does it change the amount you will get every month? Can you choose to have it pay one amount for as long as you and your spouse are alive, and some percentage of that amount when one of you dies? Does either death reduce the benefit, or only the former worker's? What other options do you have?

If you have a 401(k) plan, a profit sharing plan, or a 403(b)/TSA plan, does it have a death benefit? If so, how much is the benefit, and will it still have a death benefit after you retire?

2. Instead of the cash value of your life insurance, you need to know how much the policies will pay when you die (the net death benefit). Be sure to include any group life insurance you or your spouse has from work, and to find out whether or not that will stay in force after retirement. This is a good time to check on the beneficiary designations you have made for all your policies (who gets the money when you die), and the settlement options you have chosen (how they get it). You can get these by calling or writing to the issuing company. You should be able to find a toll-free number for the company in either the policy itself or your latest premium notice. Have your policy number handy when you call. For any work-related, company-provided insurance, again turn to your Employee Benefits or Human Resources department, or the benefits administrator, for details.

FRAILTY PLANNING

Frailty planning requires particular attention to any nursing home or long term care insurance you may already have. When did you buy it? What are the terms and benefits? Probably, the best thing to do is just to get the policy and take it with you when you meet with your planning partner.

The information you need for frailty planning is less about your own situation than it is a matter of learning about frailty and some of the options that are available for paying for frailty care. Frailty planning is more complex than either retirement income planning or estate planning, if for no other reason than because expertise is less widely distributed than it is for retirement income or estate planning.

Frailty is a complex term. In popular usage, it includes medical events that require hospitalization, such as strokes, broken hips, and heart attacks. And it includes various forms of dementia, from embarrassing or fearful times of forgetfulness to the long goodbye of Alzheimer's. It includes struggling to manage appointments, driving, or balancing the checkbook. It covers wearing Depends™ and needing help with bathing, eating, or dressing. Frailty comes on suddenly or slowly: suddenly in the event of a traumatic event, slowly in the case of the gradual decline of mind or body. Once you get there, you need help.

Popular usage generalizes "frailty" as one condition or set of circumstances. You will need to tighten the focus of this view. The healthcare and insurance industries see the frail person in precise ways, and what is considered frailty in popular discourse may not be frailty from either a healthcare or insurance perspective. In fact, one reason that we stress planning for frailty care is that we live in a country that has developed a system that responds best to acute illness or injury, and that only has widespread insurance and payment mechanisms in place for acute care. Where frailty describes a chronic condition (or set of conditions) that does not trigger traditional medical responses to acute care, mechanisms of financing and payment are not as readily available. To fund frailty care, you are basically dependent on the resources for which you are right now in the process of planning.

ACTIVITIES OF DAILY LIVING (ADLs)

It is useful for you to know how the insurance and healthcare industries understand and define frailty, because it is only under carefully defined sets of circumstances that insurance claims can be made even if you have appropriate insurance coverage. Also, it will help you to communicate with health professionals if you can speak their language. Generally, these industries describe frailty negatively, as a loss of functionality, rather than the more positive approach of relative levels of thriving.

Physical loss of functioning is commonly measured by inability to perform either Activities of Daily Living (ADLs) or Instrumental Activities of Daily Living (IADLs) without assistance, and sometimes by a standard of mobility. Loss of mental functioning is measured by standardized tests and referred to as cognitive impairment. ADLs are particularly important, because along with cognitive impairment and, in some cases, medical necessity they are the mechanism the insurance industry uses to determine qualification for long term care benefits.

Dr. Sidney Katz first defined six ADLs in the 1950s: bathing, continence, dressing, eating, toileting and transferring. These 6 ADLs are still in use today, although the definitions vary slightly—but sometimes significantly— from one long term care insurance policy to another. They measure your ability to function independently in a limited environment:

- ↬ Bathing is the ability to keep yourself clean without assistance, including the ability to take a bath or shower safely.

- ↬ Continence is your ability to maintain control of your bowels and bladder.

- ↬ Dressing is the ability to get yourself dressed, including putting on any prostheses.

- ↬ Eating is the ability to feed yourself once food is prepared and put in front of you.

- ↬ Toileting is the ability to use the toilet, including your ability to maintain personal hygiene.

- ↬ Transferring is the ability to get in and out of bed or a chair without assistance.

If you want to be able to remember what the six ADLs are, the sort-of-alphabetical mnemonic device BCDE-TT will give you the first letter of each of them.

The less standardized IADLs (Instrumental Activities of Daily Living) measure your ability to function in the community. The Mayo Clinic's shorthand here is SHAFT: shopping, housework, accounting, food preparation, and transportation. Other lists often also include the ability to do laundry, use a telephone, and manage money and medication.

What do these things have to do with how you will pay for aging? They are included for two reasons. First, to the extent that you cannot perform these functions you will need help. This is how the need for help is defined and identified. Second, to the extent that your frailty planning includes insurance benefits, ADLs—along with cognitive impairment—are the most common benefit triggers. However, the failure to be able to perform IADLs is getting some attention as a trigger in more liberal policies.

The task of gathering data for frailty planning is one of finding out what is available in the marketplace. Partly because frailty is only recently a condition that the majority of the population faces, there is neither a widely-held wisdom nor even a general understanding of either what frailty costs (except, "a lot") or what resources are available to respond to those costs. There is much confusion! The rest of the chapters of this section are designed to give you that information. You may have to share it with the professional with whom you choose to work.

Sources of Funds

There are only three potential resources for paying for frailty care: government (your tax dollars at work), wealth (your income and the money you have accumulated) and risk sharing (insurance). Which of these is best for you will depend on your personal situation but, as these are the only sources of money to pay the additional costs of frailty, you *must* think through how you will provide for your needs. This involves a clear recognition of the limits of each source, ways of accessing them, and a consideration of all options. To the extent that wealth (self-insuring) is included in your consideration, the impact on retirement and estate plans must also be accounted for.

FREE FRAILTY CARE?

You have probably noticed that we have apparently ignored support services provided by family and friends, who are known as "informal caregivers," and who help without compensation. For many people, and especially in some ethnic groups, this is the major source of frailty care. Sometimes this is by necessity, and sometimes it is by tradition. Sometimes it is for lack of any other choice, but sometimes it is by personal choice or commitment.

The world of frailty is shifting dramatically. As we noted in *The Measure of Your Days*, with medical advances people are living longer and dying sicker, usually of degenerative conditions that lead to the failure of primary body systems— slowly. Some people will tell you that in their family the elderly have always been cared for at home when they grew frail. That may well be the case. But family memories are short and imprecise. Where that was true, it was generally forty- and fifty-year-old stay-at-home women taking care of sixty- and seventy-year-old parents or relatives for a few months until they died of pneumonia or some other disease. Nowadays the scenario is more likely to be sixty- or seventy-year-olds taking care of eighty- or ninety-year-old parents for many years.

In no event is this kind of care free. We think that there is a special place in heaven for informal caregivers, and they ought not to be taken for granted, but frailty care provided by informal caregivers is not free; it just gets paid for in a currency different from dollars and cents. We do not disparage either the memories or the intent of people who talk about relying on services provided by family and friends. We do, however, challenge the adequacy of a plan grounded on that premise.

A clearly thought through and funded plan for care and support services in the frail part of life is, at the least, an essential ingredient of all of life-planning, even in the case where family will be counted on to help. Beyond that, it is fundamental to being able to live all of life with a full sense of emotional and spiritual well-being. If you get to LIKE IT OR NOT without having planned where you will live and how you will pay for help and support services, others will make decisions on your behalf. And, perhaps, they will also have to provide for your frailty care without regard for their own best interests, or yours.

CHAPTER TEN

False Hopes:
The Taxpayers' Money

False hopes may not sound like a very fair or even-handed way to begin the discussion of Medicare and Medicaid. We have chosen to characterize them this way because neither program is designed to respond to the needs we are discussing. Neither Medicare nor Medicaid is designed to provide for frailty care through the full range of responses that are commonly needed. Despite the prevailing notion that Medicare will take care of health care in old age, you must recognize that it is designed for, and is increasingly limited to, response to acute illnesses rather than chronic conditions.

Likewise, in spite of the prevailing notion that Medicaid will pay for nursing home care, that is true only in limited circumstances. In other words, Medicaid is not designed to be available to even a substantial minority of the frail, old population. And, in an era of balanced budgets, neither Medicare nor Medicaid is likely to be expanded.

In no way would we use the term "false hopes" for Medicare if we were talking about what Medicare is designed to do, namely to provide what is traditionally referred to as health care—but which never included frailty care—for senior citizens. Nor would we use the term "false hopes" for Medicaid if we were talking about what Medicaid is designed to do, namely to provide a range of health-related services for the nation's poorest citizens. Our characterization of these programs as "false hopes" has to do with what Medicare and Medicaid were not designed to do.

Changes to the design of Medicare are currently being implemented, but not the kind of changes that will increase benefits for frailty care. Medicare+Choice has six options for contracting for the delivery of acute care services. These include three types of managed care plans, a private fee-for-service plan, and Medical Savings Accounts, as well as the current plan. But none of these changes will alter the fundamental nature of Medicare as a response to acute care needs, not as a response to needs for frailty care.

While there is a growing population of people who are no longer capable of functioning independently in the world, and while these people have a high need for both health care and support services, neither Medicare nor Medicaid was designed to respond to those needs.

Medicare

Technically, Medicare is Title XVIII of the Social Security Act of 1965, as amended. As a result of its most recent amendments under the Balanced Budget Act of 1997, it now comes in three parts: Part A (Hospital Insurance), Part B (Supplemental Medical Insurance), and Part C (Medicare+Choice, which includes alternate forms of health care insurance financing: Medical Saving Accounts, managed care, etc.).

Before you doze off, let us repeat what you need to remember: Medicare is designed to provide for acute care, not chronic care.

MEDICARE AND NURSING FACILITY CARE

We get a real-life glimpse into the mismatch of Medicare with the needs of frailty care when we look at the restrictions it puts on nursing home care. In the *Guide to Health Insurance for People With Medicare*, developed jointly by the National Association of Insurance Commissioners and the Health Care Financing Administration of the US Department of Health and Human Services, you can read the following:

> Medicare Part A can help pay for up to 100 days of skilled care in a skilled nursing facility during a benefit period. All covered services for the first 20 days of care are fully paid by Medicare. All covered services for the next 80 days are paid by Medicare except for a daily coinsurance amount. The daily coinsurance in 1998 is $95.50 per day [$96.00 in 1999–ed.]. You are responsible for the coinsurance. If you require more than 100 days of care in a benefit period, you are responsible for all charges beginning with the 101st day.
>
> A skilled nursing facility is different from a nursing home. It is a special kind of facility that primarily

furnishes skilled nursing and rehabilitation services. [...] Medicare will not pay for your stay if the services you receive are primarily personal care or custodial services such as assistance in walking, getting in and out of bed, eating, dressing, bathing, and taking medicine. Medicare does not pay for custodial care if that is the only kind of care you require.[1]

Even within these boundaries, to qualify for Medicare skilled nursing care you must meet the following conditions:

1. You must have been hospitalized for three continuous days, not including the day of discharge.

2. You must be admitted to the skilled nursing facility for the same condition for which you were hospitalized. "Condition" here is a technical term that relates to the prospective payment system for hospitals and skilled nursing care facilities. It may not be the same as the way you or we would normally understand the term.

3. You must require daily skilled care that, as a practical matter, can only be provided in a facility on an inpatient basis. Given today's technology, there are not many conditions that meet that test.

MEDICARE HOSPICE BENEFITS

There is a period at the very end of life—*DYING*—when Medicare's response to acute illness also includes hospice care. This may be offered at home or in an institutional setting. Hospice care shifts the focus of medical attention from treatment of the disease to care for the comfort of the patient.

To qualify under Medicare, a patient must have a prognosis of six months or less to live if the illness runs its normal course. The average benefit period is less than two months, and most of the beneficiaries are treated in their homes.

A brief period of hospice care, no matter how compassionate, is at best only a partial answer to the long-term and complex issues of frailty care.

THE MEDICARE HOME HEALTH CARE BENEFIT

The part of Medicare you are probably most interested in here (the part that is most applicable to frailty care) is the Home Health Care Benefit. In 1967, Home Health Care accounted for 1% of Medicare expenditures of $4.2 billion dollars. By 1993, it accounted for 7% of Medicare expenditures of $142.2 billion dollars. In 1997, Congress moved to restrict the Home Health Care Benefit. (Are you really surprised?) Under the Balanced Budget Act, the definition of "Home Confinement" was tightened and the process of restricting utilization was begun as the Health Care Financing Administration (HCFA) moved toward a prospective payment system for home health care benefits similar to the system it uses for hospitals.

Some more technical jargon: there are two approaches to paying those who provide care. On the one hand, you have an indemnity or reimbursement type of system in which a service is provided and then a claim is filed and paid. It might be useful to think of this as retrospective funding of health care, because all care that is paid for has already occurred.

On the other hand, you have prospective payment systems. It might be useful to think of these as "pre-imbursement" systems. The theory behind prospective payment systems is that, based on averages and other statistical data, a provider can be paid a flat amount for the care of a group of patients in advance of providing it, and thereby given an incentive to provide care more efficiently. This is the financial technology behind HMOs. (This system is also referred to as "capitation" in some settings.) Although it is not technically correct to use this term, you might do well to think of a prospective payment system as a "prepaid health plan."

The movement to a prospective payment system for the Medicare Home Health Care benefit is the mechanism by which the government hopes to limit costs to the taxpayers. The Balanced Budget Act created a restricted interim payment system, and then replaced it with a prospective payment system (PPS) beginning in October, 1999. Altogether, a cut of about 15% in total home health spending for fiscal year 2000 (even if the PPS is delayed) was mandated.

These changes are intended to encourage agencies to improve efficiency and eliminate unnecessary services, but they run the risk of reducing access to appropriate care. Indeed, when we surveyed a group of Geriatric Case Managers (see pages 114-116), they reported a number of home health agencies going out of business and patients being forced to impoverish themselves to qualify for Medicaid. The highest users of the Medicare Home Health Care benefit, who often need a mix of acute and long term care services (that is, frailty care), are those most likely to be most dramatically affected.

There is a second way in which Congress is moving to limit Medicare's Home Health Care benefits. Part of the current "problem" is that, as a result of the Omnibus Reconciliation Act of 1980 and the 1988 *Duggan v. Bowen* settlement, caps were removed from this area of Medicare benefits. In other words, there was no limit on the Medicare Home Health Care benefit. The doctor said you needed it, you got it, and Medicare paid for it (assuming you qualified). Given the current budget climate, this will not be allowed to continue. The new system bases prospective payments on a 120 day "episode of care," with some allowance for payments beyond that in extraordinary cases.

CONCLUSION ON MEDICARE

Medicare is a fine program for what it does, but do not misunderstand what it does.

Medicare might provide some home health care services, but the focus of the program is on acute care and will remain so. Home health services make sense as a cost-effective alternative to hospitalization for acute care. But, to the extent that they are used to provide non-acute care, they are not likely to be part of Medicare's future.

You cannot rely on Medicare to pay for all, or even most of the many kinds of care and support services (frailty care) that are required for people no longer capable of independent living. That is why we call Medicare a "False Hope."

MEDICAID

Medicaid is Title XIX of the Social Security Act of 1965, as amended—most recently in the Balanced Budget Act of 1997. It is a Federal-State matching entitlement program that pays for medical assistance for certain vulnerable and needy individuals and families with very low incomes and resources. Medicaid is the largest program that funds medical and health-related services for America's poorest people. In the area of chronic health care, Medicaid does a better job for its population than Medicare does for the population at large. That is the attraction of it.

Let us get to the point: Medicaid will pay for nursing home care and, in some instances, home health care, for the impoverished. But impoverishment is a rigorously defined financial condition that differs from state to state. Generally, what it means is this: to qualify for Medicaid you will be able to keep your house, a car, a burial plot and burial funds, and a small amount of cash—ranging (depending on the state) from $1,000 to $4,000, but typically $2,000. And, when you need frailty care, you will get it in a nursing facility of the state's choosing, and the state has the right to move you.

After you have spent all but $2,000 of your assets, every cent of your income—except for about $30 a month for your incidentals—will be taken by Medicaid and paid to the nursing home. Medicaid will then make up the difference.

The impact of impoverishment on the spouse is dramatic. Obviously, your husband or wife will still need some income to live on, and Medicaid takes this into consideration. States vary on amounts, and some states—our own Virginia, for example—allow the spouse just less than $1,300 income a month. Even the most generous states allow only about $2,000 a month. Imagine trying to keep up a house or pay rent, buy heat and light, pay a cable TV bill, do maintenance, pay Medicare Part B ($45.50 a month), buy food, maintain a car, and otherwise live on this sum!

The non-institutionalized spouse will also be allowed to keep—depending on the state—a modest amount of assets (ranging from approximately $16,000 in 24 states to not quite $80,000 in 16 states). With those the limits on assets left for the spouse under the Medicaid laws, it will certainly be to Medicaid that she or he will have to turn for frailty care.

MEDICAID PLANNING

This has led some people to do what is called Medicaid Planning. Medicaid Planning is a deliberate strategy by which you become technically impoverished so that you can take advantage of Medicaid for your nursing home care without actually depriving your family of your assets.

Assets given away to individuals more than 36 months before you apply for Medicaid, or to a trust more than 60 months before, are not considered when Medicaid determines qualification. Even ignoring whether this is an ethical thing to do, it is not a painless strategy. Impoverishment is impoverishment, and most people don't want to arrive at the end of their lives either broke or dependent.

Through the 1980s and 1990s an increasing number of professionals, mostly lawyers, aggressively promoted this strategy through personal counseling and public seminars. The implications of the trend were so unacceptable to the federal and state governments that Congress criminalized the process of Medicaid Planning in the Kennedy-Kassenbaum bill of 1996 and reiterated and attempted to clarify that action again in the 1997 Balanced Budget Act.

This so-called "Send Granny to Jail" provision was neutralized by Attorney General Janet Reno who, in a letter to the Speaker of the House and other government leaders dated March 11, 1998 said, "This is to respectfully inform you that, after close and careful scrutiny of the matter, the Department of Justice will not defend the constitutionality of Section 1128B(a)(6) because the counseling prohibition in that provision is plainly unconstitutional under the First Amendment and because the assistance prohibition is not severable from the counseling prohibition." A Federal Judge in New York also found the law unconstitutional.

This may or may not be the last word on the criminalization of Medicaid Planning. However, criminalization is not the last technique that will be employed to limit the growth of Medicaid spending for frailty care. Left unchecked, Medicaid spending for long term care will bankrupt the federal and state governments. An alternative approach to limit spending that has growing popularity and is in place in many high utilization states is "income capping."

In at least 20 states, including Florida and Arizona, you cannot qualify for Medicaid at all if your monthly income is more than —at most—300% of the Supplemental Security Income (SSI) benefit, which was $500 in 1999. That means that if your gross monthly income is more than $1,500.01, you don't qualify. States can set the limit at less than 300% of SSI, but no lower than 100%. Worse, there is no spend-down provision. Under the asset test for qualification, you can "spend down" your assets until you qualify for Medicaid. In the so-called "cap states," if your income exceeds the limit, you don't qualify. There is a technique called the Miller trust that may get you around the edges of these provisions, but if that's all the income you have, you probably can't afford a lawyer to draw one up.

In a similar spirit, the 1993 Omnibus Budget Reconciliation Act (OBRA) requires states to recover the costs of long term care services from the estates of Medicaid beneficiaries. Any state that does not comply or get a waiver risks forfeiting its federal Medicaid money—which pays for about half the program. There are some exceptions, but impoverishment is impoverishment, even beyond death.

Clearly, the promoters have painted Medicaid Planning with a kind of Robin Hood charm. In this view, the poor middle class taxpayer might be seen as getting even with an oppressive rich government by forcing it to provide for his or her frailty care. There are two issues to keep in mind. First, the government has no money of its own. In reality, the poor middle class taxpayer is forcing the other middle class taxpayers to pay for his or her frail old age, not some autonomous government.

Second, remember that Robin Hood had to live in the woods. Medicaid nursing home beds are usually at or near the bottom of the list in terms of quality and desirability. While some Medicaid nursing beds are in first-class facilities, that is the exception rather than the rule. Good facilities usually charge more than Medicaid pays and they have waiting lists of private-pay clients. Remember, too, that the state (not you) chooses what nursing home you will be assigned to, and you could easily wind up 40 or 50 miles away from the community of people who know and love you.

We have dealt with the issues of impoverishment above, noting that for most people impoverishment is not an appealing prospect. Neither is the prospect of leaving your family with nothing. The choice, then, may be between intentionally impoverishing yourself by giving the money to the kids and qualifying for Medicaid, or going broke paying for the nursing home and qualifying for Medicaid. Where a Medicaid nursing home bed is the only resource for getting frailty care in THE REST OF LIVING, it is not hard to understand why some people choose to live in poverty for three or five years or longer rather than risk giving the family's modest nest egg to the nursing home. But it is not a painless choice.

---

[1]National Association of Insurance Commissioners and the Health Care Financing Administration of the US Department of Health and Human Services, *GUIDE to Health Insurance for People with Medicare*, p. 4.

CHAPTER ELEVEN

Deep Pockets: Your Money

Most frailty care in the United States is paid for out of pocket. Remember, there are only three sources of funds for frailty care: government benefits, your money, and long term care insurance. This chapter is about your money.

If you have been doing the exercises as you have read along, you have probably already added up how much money you have, or will have, to fund your aging. Given income from Social Security, pensions and annuities, as well as dividends and interest earnings on your assets, you have some sense of how much unearned income you will have to live on. You will also have a handle on how much you feel you need, and how much you will have, in reserve for emergencies or contingencies. You may have discovered that you will need to plan to spend your principal at some point to maintain your standard of living. There are undoubtedly still questions to be resolved with the help of a professional, but you have a sense of how much money you will have. You already know about stocks, bonds, mutual funds, pensions and annuities as they apply to you, or at least you have a good idea. If you are like many people we talk to, you will have either enough or not quite enough to fund a reasonable standard of living without working, but little or no reserves for emergencies.

There are two sources of money that might be available to help you fund frailty care without taking away from your retirement income or estate plans. These are often overlooked in retirement income planning. They are important assets, however, because no matter how much money you have, few people can add an expense of $4,000 or more to their budget each month without flinching. Indeed, an expense like this can even wipe you out.

HOME EQUITY CONVERSION

This section will be especially relevant if you are attracted to either HOME SWEET HOME or PROGRESSIVE RETREAT for your answer to "Where will you live?" The issue here is how to get the equity out of your house without leaving home. Our presumption is that you have a lot of equity in your house; in fact you might even have the mortgage paid off. The problem is, you don't want to sell your house to get the money out because then, where would you go? But you can't plan for funded frailty care without tapping into that money. You are house rich and cash poor.

Until a few years ago, most people had no idea how to get out of this tangle, as the only techniques available were private annuities and sale-and-lease-back programs (These techniques are still available, but are very sophisticated and complex. If you wish to consider them, please consult a lawyer skilled in this area). However, since 1989, the government has sponsored reverse mortgages, making it much easier to use the equity of your home without leaving it. With planning, average people can do what they want to do—stay in their homes *and* get the money—by using a reverse mortgage. However, reverse mortgages are still new enough that many lenders are not expert in their use and it will often take initiative on your part to avail yourself of these programs.

THE REVERSE MORTGAGE

A reverse mortgage is a loan secured by your house for which repayment is not due until after you or you and your spouse die or move out. Fannie Mae and The Federal Housing Agency (FHA) are federal agencies involved in reverse mortgages. Here's how Fannie Mae's *Money From Home* describes its reverse mortgage program.

> Unlike a traditional "home equity loan," in which your loan repayment begins as soon as you receive your loan proceeds, The Home Keeper Mortgage does not have to be repaid until you no longer occupy your home as your principal residence— that is, at the time that you sell your house, convey title or move away, or upon your death. At that time, the loan can be paid off from the proceeds of the sale of the house, or you or your heirs may keep the house if you are able to pay off the loan balance using other assets.

The amount due when your Home Keeper Mortgage becomes payable will always be the lesser of your loan balance or the market value of your property. This means that even if the amount you have borrowed eventually exceeds the value of your home, you will never owe more than the value of your home. On the other hand, if the proceeds from the eventual sale of your home exceed the amount you owe the lender, these proceeds will belong to you or your estate.[1]

Make no mistake: this is a loan, and interest accrues. That should not stop you from considering it in either of its forms—Standard and Equity Share. Standard means that the lender can never recover more than the sale price of your home. If the amount of the loan and interest is less than the value of your house, the lender will get back the smaller amount.

Equity Share means that the lender can recover the value of the loan, plus accrued interest, plus 10% of the equity in your house, up to the maximum of the sale price of your home. Equity Share is good for you because you can borrow more money on your house under this arrangement than you can in the Standard plan. What is in it for the lender is clear. If the house sells for $100,000 and the lender is owed $40,000 in principal and accrued interest, under the Standard program $40,000 is all the lender would get back. Under the Equity Share program the lender would get an additional 10% of the sale price. Thus, in our example, the lender would get $50,000 instead of $40,000. You, however, will have been able to borrow additional money.

CONSIDERATIONS

In this next section we will look at eligibility, suitability, timing, and consequences, but this description is not complete. If you are seriously considering a reverse mortgage, find several mortgage lenders that offer these products and who are skilled in explaining them. If you need names of lenders, call Fannie Mae (202) 752-7000 or write to them at 3900 Wisconsin Avenue NW, Washington, DC, 20016-2899.

ELIGIBILITY

1. There can be no more than three co-borrowers and they must all be at least 62 years old. For the purposes of a reverse mortgage, it is the age of the youngest co-borrower that is used to measure the risk for the lender. Further, if there are two co-borrowers of the same age, the amount of money yielded by the reverse mortgage will be less than if there were only one borrower—for the obvious reason that the second co-borrower might well outlive the first, and the lender will not get repaid until later.

2. You must either own your home outright or owe only a little on your mortgage The reverse mortgage must be the first mortgage, and if you have a balance remaining on your existing mortgage you will have to refinance it as part of the reverse mortgage.

3. Not every kind of house qualifies in the Fannie Mae "Home Keeper" program. Only single-family, one-unit dwellings are considered. However, in the FHA Home Equity Conversion Mortgage program (HECM), a qualifying resi-

dence can also be part of a two to four unit dwelling or a condominium in an FHA-approved development.

4. You must participate in counseling provided by either Fannie Mae or the FHA. While both require counseling, the counseling is different for each and is not interchangeable.

5. Credit worthiness is not a consideration. The loan is against the value of your property (the collateral). Neither your income nor your credit history matters.

TRUTH AND CONSEQUENCES

1. Reverse mortgages are often looked on as particularly suited to the poor who live in urban areas. While they may be appropriate in that situation, they are by no means limited to the urban poor. Nor should reverse mortgages be looked on as a desperation measure. Reverse mortgages should be considered by any homeowner who is planning for financial security throughout aging, and especially by anyone looking for an emergency or contingent resource for paying for frailty care.

2. One of the original uses of a reverse mortgage was to take the value of your house out in monthly installments to provide an income to live on. There will be those who promote the use of a reverse mortgage to acquire other financial instruments, such as immediate annuities. This might be a good idea—depending on rates— but we are suspicious and urge you always to get at least a second opinion before proceeding along these lines.

3. There are three variables in how much money you can get in a reverse mortgage: the age of the youngest borrower,

the value of the property up to a certain maximum, and the choice of either the Standard or Equity Share instrument.

a. The older the youngest borrower is, the more money you can get out of your home. The loan is not repayable until the borrower no longer lives there (which forces the repayment of the loan). The longer the time between getting the loan and its repayment, the more cost the lender bears and the more interest is owed. The lender has to anticipate that the eventual sale price of the property can cover the amount due.

b. The greater the value of the property, the more money you can get up to the program maximum (The Fannie Mae Home Keeper Program maximum is over $225,000; FHA maximums for the HECM program range from less than $90,000 to more than $170,000 across the country). The lender is staking everything on the value of the property. Your ability to repay from other sources is not an issue.

4. Watch out for scams! While not all lenders are completely familiar with reverse mortgages, there is no need to pay someone 5% to 10% of the loan amount to find one for you. There is simply no need to pay a finder's fee. If you need the name of a local lender, call Fannie Mae at 1-800-7FANNIE (1-800-732-6643), and they will send you a list.

5. A reverse mortgage is a financial decision that should not be undertaken without a great deal of thought and as part of a solid plan for financial security throughout aging. Although there is no payback requirement during your lifetime, when the money is spent it is spent. This is why there is a

counseling requirement in both the Fannie Mae and FHA programs.

RESTRUCTURING YOUR LIFE INSURANCE

As we noted at the beginning of this chapter, most frailty care in the United States is paid for out of your pocket. And most of that money comes from banking assets or stocks and bonds and mutual funds. Along with reverse mortgages, your life insurance can be a contingent source of money to pay for frailty care.

Life insurance is not anybody's most favorite topic. But stay with us: this is where you are going to learn about getting your money back instead of giving them more! Basically there are five ways you can free up money for frailty care out of life insurance:

1. Stop paying premiums and use that money for frailty care.

2. Borrow from the cash value of the policy or surrender the policy for its cash value.

3. Annuitize your life insurance policy (convert the cash value to a stream of payments).

4. Replace your existing policy with one that pays both death benefits and long term care benefits.

5. Sell your policy to a company that will give you most of the death benefit while you are still alive.

Please note: What we are suggesting has significant implications for you, your family, and your heirs. None of these steps should be taken outside the context of integrated planning for financial security throughout aging, including retirement income planning, frailty planning, and estate planning. Before you take any action, we strongly recommend that you get professional help in doing a thorough reassessment of all your life insurance policies and needs.

1. STOP PAYING PREMIUMS.

This is not just a radical suggestion. People get in the habit of paying life insurance premiums month in and month out, especially if the premiums are automatically deducted from their checking account.

When you bought your life insurance, you had a specific reason in mind: if you had died, someone may not have had enough money to live on—your spouse or your children, for example. That need may have passed by now. Your children are probably grown and on their own, and you and your spouse or partner may have accumulated enough assets to make this life insurance unnecessary.

Owning your life insurance may still serve another purpose, such as paying estate taxes. Just because the original reason you bought it has disappeared doesn't meant there is no reason to keep it. But if there is no reason to keep some or all of your life insurance, you may choose to stop paying your premiums and use the money for other things, including frailty care.

Some life insurance policies have in them a provision that allows you to stop paying premiums and still keep some death benefit. Check with the person from whom you are getting professional help in this area or call the insurance company with whom you have your policy. Most of them have toll-free numbers. With your policy number in hand, ask to speak to the customer service department to see if you are eligible for a "reduced paid-up benefit" (the technical term for what we are talking about here—having your cake and eating it too).

2. BORROW FROM THE CASH VALUE OF THE POLICY, OR SURRENDER IT FOR ITS CASH VALUE

As you know, there are two basic kinds of life insurance policies: those that are "pure" insurance (term insurance) and those that are a combination of insurance and savings (whole life, universal life, or variable life). If you have term insurance, all the money you have put in (all the premiums you have paid) has been used to pay for the death benefit protection you have had. If you had died, the policy would have paid the face amount to your beneficiary. It is like your homeowners or auto insurance—the only way you get money back is through a claim while the policy is in force.

If you have a whole life, universal life, or variable life policy, you may be able to get back some or all of the money you have paid in without having to die. There are two ways of doing this: a., you may borrow against the cash value of the policy, or b., you may surrender the policy and get the money out of it. Both options have pros and cons.

a.   Borrowing against the policy has a significant plus: it leaves the policy in force. That is, you still have some life insurance death benefit payable when you die, equal to the face amount of the policy minus whatever you have borrowed from it. The minuses are:

↭ You will continue to have to pay premiums, and

↭ You will have to pay interest on what you have borrowed.

b. Surrendering the policy for its cash value also has pros and cons. The biggest plus is that you get all your money out and you don't have to pay any more premiums. The minus is evident: you no longer have any life insurance under this policy. Less evident, perhaps, is the fact that you are likely to have to pay some income tax on the amount you get back.

3. Annuitize Your Life Insurance Policy

All whole life, variable life, and universal life insurance policies have what is called an "annuity option." This means that you can use the cash value of the policy to buy an annuity: a guaranteed periodic (usually monthly) check paid to you. You have some choice about how long this will be paid—a "life only" option (payments for as long as you live), a "joint and survivor" option (payments for as long as you or your spouse or partner lives), or payments for a minimum guaranteed period (e.g. payments for your lifetime or at least 10, 15, or 20 years). What choice you make dramatically affects how much money you get in each payment.

Every policy has written into it guaranteed rates that will tell you (maybe with the aid of an interpreter) how much you will be paid each month per thousand dollars of cash value for each annuity option. If you bought your policy at a time when interest rates were high, you should get substantially more money in each check than if you bought the policy when interest rates were low. You may get more money in each monthly check by surrendering the policy and using the money to buy the best available annuity on the open market. But don't overlook annuitizing your policy—it may be the best rate available and you won't have to pay another commission.

4. REPLACE YOUR LIFE INSURANCE POLICY WITH ONE THAT PAYS BOTH DEATH BENEFITS AND LONG TERM CARE INSURANCE BENEFITS

At least three companies offer life insurance policies that take into account the economic impact of frailty care. These policies pay your beneficiary the full face amount of the policy if you die without having used them to pay for frailty care. If you do not go through the LIKE IT OR NOT transition into THE REST OF LIVING, these policies will be no different from any others. But, they also pay for frailty care—under very specific terms and conditions—if you can no longer function independently. In the latter case, they pay a (much) smaller death benefit when you die.

Assuming that you meet the physical and mental requirements of the new company, and qualify, you will be able to transfer the cash value of your existing policy (or policies) to this new plan without having to pay income tax. Technically this is called a Section 1035 exchange. The rules for doing it are very precise. Beware! Do not proceed without professional assistance!

5. SELL THE POLICY

If the insured under a life insurance policy is certified by a physician to be within six months of death, almost all policies (whenever written) allow you to claim most or all of the death benefit, either in a lump sum or in monthly payments over that period, under some form of an "accelerated death benefit" provision. Policies written before the late 1980s are not likely to have this provision written in them, but most companies will issue a rider or accommodate you by administrative practice.

What happens if you have a terminal illness but you are expected to live more than six months, or your life insurance policy does not have an "accelerated death benefit" provision? There is an alternative called a "viatical settlement." In a viatical settlement, you sell a policy on your life to somebody else, for less than the face amount. You get the money now—while you are very much still alive. How much you might get for the policy will be a function of the face value of the policy (the death benefit), whatever has been borrowed from the policy, how long you are expected to live, how much the buyer will have to pay in premiums, and prevailing interest rates. After the transaction, the purchaser pays the premiums and gets the full face amount when death ultimately occurs.

Very recently, some companies (not life insurance companies!) have started to offer to buy the "excess insurance" of people who are neither within six months of dying nor suffering a terminal illness. For the most part, anyone over age 65 can find a buyer for any insurance on their life. Whatever the circumstance, you get a percentage of the death benefit while you are alive and can use it to pay for frailty care.

There are two reasons why the option of a viatical settlement might be important. First, under the financial stress of frailty care, the burden of paying life insurance premiums may be so great that the person has to give up the life insurance policy altogether. If the coverage is term insurance, or was purchased recently, this may be particularly problematic as there will be no cash value to get back. Second, the money that comes from a viatical settlement may provide the financial resources for quality frailty care.

Our treatment of these five options does not exhaust the considerations of your particular situation. To repeat: what we are suggesting has significant implications for you, your family, and your heirs. This is definitely part of both frailty and estate planning, and should not be done in isolation. Before you take any action, we strongly recommend that you get professional help in doing a thorough-going reassessment of all your life insurance policies and needs.

CHAPTER TWELVE

Shared Risk: Other Peoples' Money

LONG TERM CARE INSURANCE (LTCI)

The costs of frailty care are both unpredictable and potentially devastating. One way you can manage the risk of not having enough money for frailty care is by buying insurance that pays for medical and support services when you can no longer function independently. Such policies are called long term care insurance, or LTCI. Long term care insurance is insurance that pays for frailty care. That is, LTCI pays for medical and support services not covered by acute health care insurance such as Medicare. And, while it is distinct from coverage for acute health care, it must be distinguished from "nursing home insurance"—an older form of insurance that only covers care in a nursing home.

Insurance is based on the laws of large numbers. None of us as individuals can predict what will happen to us, and most will not have enough money to pay for all the horrible things that might happen to us. But it is possible to predict what will happen to all of us together and what it will cost, and to spread those costs over a large number of us. Thus, if a lot of us pay a relatively small amount (an insurance "premium") into a common pool (the "reserves" of an insurance company), any individual who participates in the pool (a policyholder) and suffers a loss will be able to draw on many other people's money to meet that loss.

Another benefit is that, at least with the best LTCI coverages, you get plugged into a network of expertise that coordinates care, assures that you are treated with the best practices available locally, and monitors your care. In this way, the best LTCI policies go beyond the traditional definition of risk as a lack of money, and expand the notion of risk to include lack of access to excellence.

What you are trying to buy with LTCI is sustained expert involvement when you can no longer function independently, expert involvement that is sympathetic both to you and to your community of support. At the point of claim, neither you nor your community of support are likely to be prepared with expertise—and will certainly be unprepared because of emotional trauma—to make the myriad decisions that are required. All that you will know for sure is that you need help. Money is important, but by itself is insufficient to the task.

Long term care insurance is complex, and is not yet widely supported by well-trained and knowledgeable agents. As we said, the task of gathering the facts of your situation for frailty planning is one of finding out what is available, and in this case that means knowing enough about LTCI to determine whether, when, and at what cost LTCI is good for you, and what to look for if you choose to buy some. You will learn that in the rest of this chapter.

IS LONG TERM CARE INSURANCE GOOD FOR YOU?

1. Whether LTCI is good for you depends in part on how you have answered the "Where will you live?" question. The only "Where will you live?" strategic choice that makes the purchase of LTCI completely unwise is the version of THE LAST RESORT that includes an extensive coverage contract. Remember? That is the decision to move to a continuing care retirement community or life care community with an extensive agreement payment structure. Those are the contracts that provide for everything forever after you have paid a fee up front and while you continue to pay the community's standard monthly fee for your housing unit.

2. Another aspect of determining whether LTCI is good for you is knowing what other resources you have for paying for frailty care. You should now understand that in most cases neither Medicare nor Medicaid provides a reliable source of funds for frailty care, and very few people are wealthy enough to add $4,000 or more to their monthly budget. Those that do have that kind of wealth often recognize that sharing the risk of such a financial burden makes better economic sense than self-insuring. LTCI clearly does not make sense if your income is such that paying the premium will interfere with daily living.

WHEN IS LTCI GOOD FOR YOU?

When to buy long term care insurance is not clear cut. The major issues are whether you can buy it, the impact of your age at issue on the premiums, and whether the LTCI you choose will continue to suit your needs in a dynamic and developing field.

TIMING

The first issue is timing. You can't just walk in off the street and say, "I'll take some of that stuff." You have to qualify medically for LTCI and "they don't insure burning houses!" You may already have a medical condition that makes you ineligible to buy LTCI. Insurers are not fools. They want to sell you their product but they are constantly trying to assess the risk your particular health realities represent so that they do not commit too much of other people's money (or their profits) to you.

Further, even if you are healthy enough to qualify today, there will come a day when you can no longer buy it, even if you want to, because you will not qualify medically. Unfortunately, no one can identify that day except by looking backwards. Trying to time your purchase for the day before you become ineligible is playing Russian roulette with your well-being and the well-being of your spouse or partner and all those who love you. It is not possible to know in advance when the day will come when you will not qualify. The challenge is to select the best trade-off between buying too soon (paying premiums longer than absolutely necessary) and waiting too long (past the point when you can qualify to buy LTCI, or need to file a claim).

THE IMPACT OF AGE ON PREMIUMS

The second issue is the impact of age on premiums. The way the premium structure works in general is this: long term care insurance premiums stay level; they don't go up from year to year. Technically, the company reserves the right to raise the rate for an entire class of policyholders, state by state, with the approval of the state's insurance department. In such a case, the company would have to justify the amount of the rate increase with actuarial evidence. Even were premiums to be increased for an entire class of policyholders, they would then stay level at the new rate.

As a general rule, if you were to price the identical policy at ages 55, 65, and 75 you would find that the annual premium is roughly twice as much at age 65 as at age 55, and roughly three times as much at age 75 as at age 65. One policy we examined worked out this way: for a $150 per day unlimited benefit, at age 55 the annual premium is $930. For the identical coverage at age 65, the annual premium is $1,860. Waiting until age 75 to buy the same coverage—assuming you can still qualify to buy it—raises the annual premium to $5,355.

Take a moment to work out the timing issues. Let's say that you and your twin brother discuss LTCI when you are 55. You buy it now, but he decides to wait until he is 65. He figures that by age 75 you will both have spent the same amount— $18,600. Not really.

There are three significant differences that the numbers don't reveal. The first is obvious, but easy to overlook: you will have been insured for ten years longer. The second is not quite so obvious: there is no guarantee that he will be able to buy it. Health changes. The third takes more thought: any good policy purchased at age 55 will have a 5% per year compound inflation rider, and ten years out will be worth 155% of what you bought. Your brother faces a difficult choice—buy what you started with and never catch up or catch up in benefits by paying a much higher premium.

WAITING FOR BETTER COVERAGES TO BE DEVELOPED

A third question is whether, in the dynamic and developing field of frailty care and long term care insurance, you should wait to buy LTCI until the situation stabilizes. There is no need to do that if you buy intelligently.

First, good policies that you buy today include ways of modifying their benefits to accommodate changes. This provision is referred to as an "alternate plan of care" benefit, or words to that effect, and is specifically designed to anticipate paying claims for frailty care practices which don't exist today. It is true that the technology of frailty care is changing rapidly, and today's "best practices" may be tomorrow's "remember whens." For example, "assisted living" didn't exist ten years ago; who knows what will exist ten years from now that we can't imagine today? How such a provision is worded, and what restrictions it has, are obviously important technical considerations, but you should only consider buying an LTCI policy that has such a provision.

Second, the industry does try to accommodate change without requiring replacement. For example, ever since income tax deductibility of LTCI premiums and the tax-free nature of qualified LTCI benefits were first defined under the 1996 Health Insurance Portability and Accountability Act (HIPAA), there has been confusion over whether a "tax-qualified" or "non-tax-qualified" policy would be better because of other provisions in the law that restrict benefit triggers. HIPAA made all contracts issued before January 1, 1997 tax-qualified without requiring them to meet the new rules, so anybody who had gone ahead and made the purchase got the best of both worlds. And companies generally gave their policyholders a year to make a decision whether they wanted TQ (tax qualified) or NTQ (non-tax-qualified) policies while rules were being formulated and new policy forms were being approved by the states.

Finally, if you had bought what passed for LTCI ten years ago, all you would have been able to cover would have been care in a nursing home. In all likelihood you would be better off with one of the more comprehensive policies available today, and you should consider upgrading your coverage (but only with the assistance of a well qualified specialist in LTCI). Should you have waited to buy? No, because the need to pay for care could well have developed in the interim, or you could have become uninsurable. In either case, even the old nursing home policy would have been great LTCI insurance! The best policy is always the one that is in force and pays claims when you need them.

At What Cost is LTCI Good for You?

There is no rule of thumb that provides an answer, but there is a way to ask the question—namely in terms of the relationship of costs to benefits, a "cost/benefit analysis." Frailty care is expensive, and having insurance to pay for it can be a key piece in providing financial security throughout aging. That's the benefit. But funding frailty care with long term care insurance also costs money. That's the cost. So, the way to ask the question is this: given your financial circumstances, is the cost of LTCI going to outweigh the potential benefit?

At one end of the scale, that question translates to, "Is it going to make living so financially uncomfortable that buying LTCI is just not worth it?" In this case, the problem lies in not having enough money to both pay for LTCI and to live the way you want to. Clearly, if you are financially on the margins, you are probably better forming a strategy for frailty care based on Medicaid paying the bill. At the other end of the scale, if you are financially comfortable—that is, if the LTCI premium is not going to be a cost that even affects your budget for living—then the cost is low enough for you to consider buying long term care insurance.

The issue is trickier if you are financially in-between (that is, for most people). The temptation is to say that if LTCI is not easily affordable it is not a good choice. Maybe that is so for some, but we think if you are in this situation you especially need to consider LTCI. You have something to protect (so Medicaid is not a first choice) but not so much to protect or rely on that the cost of LTCI is not an issue. This does not rule out LTCI; rather it calls for a lot of honest conversation, good counsel, and some creativity.

For example, let's say that you are planning to use a combination of THE FAMILY PLAN and the equity in your house to cover frailty care when you pass through LIKE IT OR NOT into THE REST OF LIVING. Let's say that you have talked this over seriously with your adult children. But now someone is trying to sell you some LTCI. Should you buy it? Maybe, and maybe not. Don't dismiss it out of hand. Get your adult children—your prospective caregivers—into the discussion.

It may be that having LTCI gives your adult children (and their spouses) the breathing room they need to agree freely and wholeheartedly to be caregivers. We suspect that a lot of adult children say "yes" to THE FAMILY PLAN because they love their parents, but that their real doubts and fears don't come out until their heads hit the pillows and they are talking to their spouses. Knowing that they will not be relied upon to provide all the care—that there will be money available to provide for increasing levels of care if and as independent functioning declines—may make THE FAMILY PLAN a joyful experience rather than a duty driven by guilt. Maybe having long term care insurance will make it possible to keep the equity in the house as a reserve, and make it possible to use that money to support a grandchild's college tuition.

Perhaps your adult children would be willing to share the cost of the premiums for LTCI rather than have to carry the entire care load on their shoulders later. This is a sophisticated form of the Fram™ oil filter "pay me now or pay me later" choice. Perhaps the adult children who cannot or will not agree to share their homes and lives will agree to share the premiums so as to lighten the load on the siblings who will

Thriving After 55 ∽

have Mom and Dad under their roof. They also serve who only pay the premium...

Issues in selecting Long Term Care Insurance.

Long term care insurance is complex, technical, often confusing, and unlike any other form of insurance. LTCI is especially unlike any other insurance in terms of the poignancy of the claim. That puts demands on the insurance companies that only a few have willingly accepted. If you choose to buy LTCI, you want to buy the product that is the best for you, from a company that understands frailty care and is committed to being your partner in that venture.

The following ten issues are critically important in making your decision:

1. Does the agent know aging?
2. Is the company sound?
3. How are claims managed?
4. Is the policy treatment plan neutral?
5. Is the policy future-proof?
6. What triggers benefits?
7. What provisions are made to prevent lapses?
8. Is this an indemnity or reimbursement style policy?
9. Is there a home modification benefit?
10. What are the pricing biases?

You should get answers to these questions in your discussion with a knowledgeable agent. You *will not* get them from advertising brochures. You *will* get them from reading LTCI policies. Under no circumstances should you ever purchase a policy without reading and understanding it. This is not car insurance. This is an integral part of your planning to thrive for the whole of your life. If you can't understand it now, with your full faculties, you have no hope of understanding it when claim time comes.

Be grown-up in your purchasing. If the product looks too good to be true, it almost certainly is. If, for example, a policy offers a 50% discount when both spouses buy policies, or if the company will underwrite absolutely anyone, or if the company promises that it will be Mother Theresa herself who will care for you . . . Well, you get the idea. What we said earlier about the stability of premiums does *not* apply if you buy LTCI that is too good to be true.

1. DOES THE AGENT KNOW AGING?

You don't deal directly with a company; you deal first with an agent. An agent who doesn't understand aging cannot give you objective, knowledgeable advice. You need your agent to demonstrate a clear understanding of aging and frailty care, not just insurance. How will you know?

Ask the agent if he or she is a member of the National Council on the Aging (NCOA) or the American Society on Aging (ASA) or United Seniors Health Cooperative (USHC). Those are all organizations committed to vital aging in the country, and membership in one or more is an indicator that the agent is committed to staying up-to-date in the field. Ask about his or her continuing education in the area of aging. Ask if the agent has ever volunteered with any organization that reaches out to the frail. Get a feel for the agent's character and comfort level with—or fear of—frailty. Fear is a little dark room where negatives are developed. An agent who is negative about frailty cannot serve you well in planning for it.

Ask what the local Area Agency on Aging (AAA) can do for you should you become frail. Ask the agent about care providers in your area; ask what the agent thinks of two or three facilities or organizations with which you are familiar. Bluntly, if the agent doesn't know the difference between the Home Health Care benefit of Medicare and Meals on Wheels, or what Medicaid is likely to provide and under what conditions, that agent does not know aging.

Then satisfy yourself that the person across the desk or table from you is staying current with the LTCI marketplace. One minimum sign of this will be that the agent represents at least three or four quality companies that insure for frailty care. Different companies skew their products to different market segments and price them differently. An agent who represents only one company routinely will represent your interests only secondarily. Ask what product changes or enhancements the agent has most recently added to or dropped from his or her portfolio of offerings, and why.

2. IS THE COMPANY SOUND?

The best LTCI policy in the world is worthless if the company that wrote it is insolvent, that is, is no longer able to pay claims when you need it to pay yours. Solvency is a technical matter that you can best get a read on by consulting various rating services. Rating services such as A. M. Best Company, Standard and Poor's, Moody's, and Weiss are companies who have made it their business to assess the claims paying ability and solvency of financial institutions. An agent should present the ratings of all companies being proposed for your consideration. Not all companies are rated by all rating agencies, and you need not draw any conclusion from the fact that one or another rating agency does not rate the insurance company you are considering. Neither should you draw any positive conclusion about the company rated beyond its solvency and claim-paying ability.

The table below shows you what to look for, comparatively, one rating company to another. This is important, as A+ from one company does not mean the same as A+ from another.

Description	A.M. Best	Standard & Poor's	Moody's	Weiss
Very High Ratings	A++ A+	AAA AA+	Aaa Aa1	A+ A A-
High Ratings	A+(c) A, A(c) A-	AA AA-	Aa2 Aa3	B+ B
Good Ratings	A-(c) B++, B+ B+(c)	A+ A-	A1 A2 A3	B- C+

Weiss' ratings are particularly helpful (especially to Henry, a long-time teacher, who is suspicious of anyone who gives all A's!). Companies with ratings below what's in the table should be regarded with great caution.

3. How are claims managed?

A care coordinator (sometimes known as a geriatric case manager) is a person—generally with a nursing or social work background—who assesses your situation and your level of functioning and puts together a plan of care that is best for you. This person must know local care providers and community services intimately, with their strengths and weaknesses, in order to create a plan that is both cost-effective and personally appropriate.

Provisions for care coordination in LTCI policies fall on a continuum from "none at all" through "claims manager" to "care coordinator as gate-keeper" to "personal advocate."

"None at all" is undesirable.

A "claims manager" who is an employee of the insurance company is not a care coordinator in the way we use the term here, although some companies will try to pass them off as such. It is not unreasonable for you to be concerned whether a company employee will put your best interests ahead of the corporate bottom line.

Most policies that provide for care coordinators at all use an approach that casts the care coordinator in the role of "gate keeper." That may or may not be the intent, but it is often the effect. In this situation, the care coordinator is contracted directly by the insurance company. This can be a very good situation. A care coordinator that does a lot of work for one company will know the policy benefits and can put together a hassle-free and effective care plan. And such a person is much more independent than a company's claim manager. On the other hand, it cannot go unnoticed that people who get a significant percentage of their business from one source, such as an insurance company, may not feel completely free of economic pressure to conform to standards or guidelines.

"Care coordinator as personal advocate" means that the insurance company will pay for—but otherwise will have nothing to do with selecting or supervising—the person who speaks for you. The insurance company is likely to require that your personal advocate be a registered nurse, a social worker, an employee of an agency that provides care management services, or a licensed or certified healthcare professional who can review, evaluate, and provide advice on your care needs. That is not unreasonable, since all parties have to speak the same language so that they can communicate easily. There are currently relatively few policies that will pay for this style of care coordinator. Increasingly, we believe, better policies will offer this benefit, either alone or in conjunction with claims managers.

This is not an unalloyed benefit. To take full advantage of this kind of benefit, you must take steps to be known by someone who can fill this role when you can no longer function independently. Our conclusion is, take your future care coordinator to lunch while you can both enjoy it!

Ultimately, any treatment plan—regardless of who develops it—must work within the structure of your LTCI policy if you want the insurance company to pay for it. Insurance policies govern benefits, and nothing else. Still, the extent to which you are represented by someone who is free to be your advocate as aggressively as necessary may be the extent to which you and your community of support get the specific benefits that you have paid premiums for, tailored to meet your particular desires and demands.

4. IS THE POLICY TREATMENT PLAN NEUTRAL?

A treatment plan neutral policy pays for care wherever it is appropriate—either in your home, in places such as Adult Day Care centers, or in facilities such as assisted living or nursing homes. Such a policy allows the benefit to be for care in whatever place best suits you.

What is at stake is whether your policy or your best interests will dictate your care plan. A policy that is treatment plan neutral does not pay a different rate for nursing home care and home care. This is important. If the policy were to pay $150/day for nursing home care and only $75/day for home health care, guess where you're going. The difference in payment structure might determine where you are cared for, regardless of your personal needs and wants. At the very least, if your LTCI is not treatment plan neutral it will present your care coordinator with an economic dilemna. If you have chosen THE LAST RESORT as your answer to the "Where will you live?" question, a policy that covers only facility-based care may be the exception to this rule.

5. IS THE POLICY FUTURE-PROOF?

"Future-proof" refers to three issues: cost, treatment plan, and regulation.

First, cost. We don't know how much frailty care will cost in the future, but we are certain it will be more expensive than it is today. The way you protect against increasing costs is to buy benefits that increase over time. The mechanism for this is to put an inflation rider on your policy. Generally speaking, there are four options:

a. *Five percent (5%) per year, compound.* This means that each year, on the anniversary of the policy, the benefit to you increases by 5% of what it was the previous year, without any increase in your premium. Thus, for example, if your daily benefit starts at $150 it will be $157.50 in year two, $165.37 in year three, $173.64 in year four, and so on. We strongly recommend this 5% compound type of future-proofing, and would require it for anyone under 65 if we could.

b. *Five percent (5%) per year, simple.* This means that each year, on the policy anniversary, the benefit to you increases by 5% of the base benefit without any increase in your premium. Thus, for example, if your daily benefit starts at $150 per day, it will increase by $7.50 per day each year. In the early years of a policy, the difference between compound and simple inflation riders is not dramatic. So, a simple interest rider might be acceptable for someone in their mid-70s or older. Beyond twelve years, the differences escalate. We urge you to think carefully before choosing this option.

c. *Inflation rider tied to the Consumer Price Index (CPI)*. This means that your benefit will increase at the same rate as the Consumer Price Index. This is better than nothing, but still not acceptable. The Medical Price Index is rising much faster than the more general CPI.

d. *No inflation rider*. This means just what it says. It is only acceptable for someone who is buying a policy in his or her mid to late 80s or older. Even then, it takes careful consideration before you decide to save the extra premium for an inflation rider.

Some policies offer you the guaranteed right to buy additional benefits, usually every two years. This is a valuable benefit, but should be considered along with an inflation rider, not instead of it.

The second issue in future-proofing is treatment plan. Frailty care is a fast-developing field. As much as possible, you want the policy to cover not only the forms of care that we already know about and those that are being developed, but also everything we can't see coming.

The provision in an LTCI policy that covers this is called something like the "Alternate Plan of Care" benefit. You want to be sure that this is written broadly enough to include as-yet-undeveloped forms of care. For example, assisted living facilities barely existed in 1990. In 1995, Massachusetts had fewer than a dozen; in 1999 it had over 115 with more under construction. In the early 1990s, nursing homes covered a range of care from skilled nursing down to help with activities of daily living, and were the primary setting for all facility-based care. At this point in time—except in the case of Medicaid beds—

nursing homes increasingly do nothing but skilled nursing care. Today, support in THE REST OF LIVING is primarily provided in assisted living facilities. Ten years from now, who knows what technologies of care will be available? You want your policy to be as open to the future as is possible.

Third, regulation. In the late 1990s, this came up frequently as a debate over whether to buy tax-qualified (TQ) or non-tax-qualified (NTQ) long term care insurance. The issue first arose in 1996, when the Federal Government formally defined long term care insurance for tax purposes. This generated some advantages: the benefits of TQ policies are income tax free and, to some extent (based on age), the premiums are tax deductible. It also generated some disadvantages: benefit triggers became more restrictive.

Cases can be made for both TQ and NTQ policies, although our clear preference is for tax qualified LTCI. The momentum of regulation of LTCI is formidable and is unlikely to be reversed. Unquestionably, the government is relying on its citizens to take care of their own frailty care because proposals that would put Washington in the frailty care business are expensive. It does not follow, however, that the IRS is likely to grant tax-free status to the benefits of policies that do not conform to their regulations. And, while any expense incurred *may* be a deductible offset to any income generated from benefits, it also may not be. Therefore, be leery of anyone who counts on a change in the direction of federal regulation of this issue to justify their position.

6. WHAT TRIGGERS BENEFITS?

Generally, what triggers benefits is that you become unable to function independently in the world. This can be either because of physical limitations or because of cognitive impairment. What matters is how the LTCI policy defines that. Physical limitations are measured by Activities of Daily Living (ADLs): bathing, continence , dressing, eating, toileting, and transferring (getting from bed to chair, etc.). Most policies include all six of these, and trigger benefits on the inability to perform two or more of the six activities.

A few policies trigger benefits on three out of the six ADLs. They are not a good choice. Some exclude bathing, which is normally the first ADL that people cannot perform. A policy that triggers benefits on 2 out of 5 ADLs, but doesn't include bathing, is really a policy that triggers benefits on 3 out of 6 ADLs.

Cognitive impairment is measured by specific clinical tests that determine a loss of intellectual capacity which places you in jeopardy of harming yourself or others unless you receive assistance. These benefit triggers function equally regardless of where care is to be provided. At least in tax-qualified policies, this trigger is quite consistent across companies.

Prior to the Health Insurance Portability and Accountability Act of 1996, most policies included a provision that would trigger benefits based on "medical necessity." If you are considering a non-tax-qualified LTCI policy because it includes a medical necessity trigger, you need to weigh the trade-offs extremely carefully.

7. WHAT PROVISIONS ARE MADE TO PREVENT LAPSES?

What happens if you don't pay your premium on time? People who are somewhat frail but not yet in need of the kind of frailty care provided for by LTCI may well forget to make a premium payment. Or, they could be off on a six-month, around the world cruise. Whatever the case, the policy you buy should provide for a lapse period of 65 days with third party notification. This means that when the payment is overdue after 30 days, the company then mails a second premium notice to you, and a notice to another person that you have designated (such as an adult child, a friend, or whoever has your power of attorney). The company allows five days for the mail to get to this person (or institution) and 30 more days for payment to be made.

In such policies, there is no talk of having to "reinstate" a policy when it is paid within the 65 day grace period. Other policies are less clear—and less desirable.

8. INDEMNITY OR REIMBURSEMENT STYLE POLICY?

An "indemnity" policy is one that, when you qualify for benefits, pays you the full benefit amount regardless of how much you pay or are charged for services. A "reimbursement" policy is one that, when you qualify for benefits, pays you for the actual costs of covered services you incur, up to a daily or weekly limit.

The advantage of an indemnity policy is that, if your covered costs are less than the benefits, you have extra money to pay for non-covered costs such as housekeeping or massage or whatever. On the other hand, the duration of benefits sets rigid limits. If you have a two year benefit period, on the 731st day it is done.

On the other hand, with a reimbursement-style policy, in most cases if your covered costs are less than the benefit amount, you don't get the difference paid to you, but you don't lose it, either. The difference is kept in a benefit bank account, to be used as covered costs are incurred—no matter how long that takes. What is rigid in these policies is not the duration of claims, but rather the maximum benefit amount. This is calculated by multiplying the daily maximum times the "duration" of coverage—and then you can forget about how long your policy will last. It will last as long as you are alive, qualified to receive benefits, and there is money in the policy.

Which is better? Neither, but they are very different in actual practice. If you buy an indemnity-style policy with a short duration, you must pay attention to your personal reserves of available funds in case THE REST OF LIVING outlasts the policy. If you buy a benefit bank account reimbursement-style policy, the construction of your plan of care must be very much more sensitive to what you use policy benefits for, so as to stretch it as far as possible.

9. IS THERE A HOME MODIFICATION BENEFIT?

If the best plan of frailty care for you is going to be in your home, or the home of a family member, it is likely that the house will need some modifications: a ramp, or an elevator, or a wheelchair accessible bathroom. Who is going to pay for these modifications? Some LTCI policies include benefits that will pay these expenses along with daily charges for services—but not all.

If you want this kind of benefit, make sure it is part of the policy you buy. If the company from which you are considering buying LTCI does not include this, or offer it as an option, and you could not otherwise purchase the modifications you need, you may need to look elsewhere for your insurance. If you can't use your own bathroom, you know you will wind up in a nursing home.

10. WHAT ARE THE PRICING BIASES?

One of the reasons we urge you to deal with an agent who represents many companies is that every company has different biases in their pricing. Some companies offer couples significantly better rates than singles. Some offer "preferred" or "substandard" rates; some only accept or reject applicants at their one published rate. Some have premiums that are more favorable at younger ages than their competitors; others are better at older ages.

The pricing bias you are most likely to see is the so-called "spousal discount." There are two questions here: how is "spousal" defined, and how does it affect the cost of the policies?

Many companies offer a discount when both spouses buy policies. These discounts typically range from 10% to 20%. Why? Because the companies know that if you have someone else at home to help with care this will likely defer the onset of the claim and lessen their costs of care. They have also figured out that people living together are, at least statistically, better health risks.

A key issue is how "spousal" is defined. A few companies have expanded the notion of "spousal" to include a partner or companion other than a legal spouse. This has nothing to do with sexual orientation. It simply notes that two people living together who are committed enough to staying together to buy LTCI policies together also have each other at hand to help with frailty care.

Another issue is how the spousal benefit affects the cost of the policy. Usually it goes this way: a company that does not offer a discount for spouses or partners will offer better rates for a single person.

The question, "At what cost is LTCI good for you?" needs to be answered in the context of a broad consideration of costs and benefits that includes the whole human context in which you age, and all three legs of the stool of financial security: retirement income planning, frailty planning and estate planning. This is a compelling reason to do the work suggested in this book, and to build the practical foundation to support fully living the rest of your life.

It is also a compelling argument for every one of us to be involved in our communities. Bluntly, your own self-interest is best served by serving others, because what goes around does come around. LTCI may or may not be part of determining whether you enjoy a sense of financial security throughout aging, but how you live will determine whether you thrive.

How Will You Live?

At the beginning of this book we said that aging happens, and that how it happens is a variable that is up to you. We know that, left to happen on its own terms, aging can be outrageously and unnecessarily expensive in both dollars and cents and in more profound human currencies. We also know that if you will turn now to the task of getting ready to thrive for all of your life, it is possible to fully live right through to life's last breath.

How do we know that? And what does it mean to thrive in the face of the real and palpable losses of frailty?

First, how do we know that it is possible to thrive to life's last breath? Because we—all of us—have seen people who have done it. These thrivers have developed, flourished, grown, succeeded, taken root where they were, even though they were in places we could hardly imagine ourselves, even though their bodies—and even their minds—were no longer their familiar life-long friends. They did not fail, languish, pine, or wither in spite of daunting challenges. These people experience the present as full of interest and providing many satisfactions; they have not given in to the stereotype that the last stages of life cannot be times of satisfaction and contentment.

A group of people from ages 73-93 was asked, "Looking back, what period of your life brought you the most satisfaction?" Almost a third of them indicated their satisfaction with the present time. The author of the study commented, "It was quite unexpected that so many old persons expressed such positive feelings about the present time."[1] She captured her own sense of conviction about this in a brief verse she quotes from Wu-men, an ancient Zen master:

Ten thousand flowers in spring, the moon in autumn,
A cool breeze in summer, snow in winter.
If your mind isn't clouded by unnecessary things,
This is the best season of your life.

This brings us to the second question, "What does it mean to thrive in the face of the real and palpable losses of frailty?" Certainly it has something to do with not having a mind clouded by unnecessary things. For example, if the only way you can imagine to be old is to be young, your mind is indeed clouded by unnecessary—and impossible—illusions!

So, what does it mean? Even in the face of declining resources, there are unique, resilient ways of adapting in later life. Techniques of selection (doing what you can), optimization (doing it as well as you can) and compensation (finding alternate ways to get it done) can be brought to bear in all areas of living. For some, this is accomplished by rearranging values, setting more modest goals, and adjusting hopes and wants to fit with given situations. It is putting into practice the Shaker song:

> 'Tis a gift to be simple,
> 'Tis a gift to be free,
> 'Tis a gift to come down where we ought to be [...]
> When true simplicity is gained,
> To bow and to bend we shan't be ashamed.

For some, accommodation comes by focusing attention away from what causes pain and onto what is positive. "No, my health isn't what I'd like it to be," an old friend said, "but I don't dwell on it. I've got lots to be thankful for." With that she pointed to a ray of sun playing on the flower by her bed. This is not denial; it can be better described as "gating"—choosing what will and what will not get in.

Thriving in the midst of real and palpable losses can also take the form of strategies of change. Change can be self-change, such as exercising to increase strength, studying to increase competence, or adopting a "new look" to increase personal attractiveness. For a few, change can also take the form of a mission to change society. Doris Haddock found herself in desperate need of a mission when her best friend died. Her Home Page on the internet reads:

> "I'm Granny D, and in my 89th year, I am walking across America from California to Washington, DC. [...] Call me crazy, call me God-sent, I am on a crusade. My purpose is to create a groundswell for Campaign Finance Reform to eliminate the cancer [of soft money]."[2]

Thriving to your last breath, or fully living the rest of your life, is not some "Pollyannaish" dream. The myth that the last years of life are spent in isolation, discomfort, and loneliness must be confronted by experiences of people who thrive. Put the myth to rest. Don't deny in the darkness what you have seen in the light!

Those who age successfully have learned to deal with life as life is, and others as others are. Even in restrictive environments or when hobbled by ill health, they respond to life, make conscious choices when they can and deal with constraint when they have to. These are people who live creatively no matter what their life circumstances, and who transcend the inevitable limitations of human existence. For some of these people, this is a new-found freedom; for others it is a life-long habit.

Your answers to the questions "Where will you live?" and "How will you pay for it?" are two of the foundations for thriving. While those answers are fundamental, they do not exhaust the question of what really counts in the long run: thriving.

Thriving minimizes the cost to your self and others in human currencies. To the extent that you live all of your life, down to the very last breath, you and those who love and support you will not pay heavy prices in psychological pain or spiritual agony. Thriving inspires.

Thriving maximizes the payoff of a life well lived for you and your community of support. Those who thrive not only in EXTENDED MIDDLE AGE, but right through READY OR NOT, THE

NEW ME, *LIKE IT OR NOT*, THE REST OF LIVING and *DYING* give the greatest gift a person can give: reflecting what it means to live, rather than to just exist. Even Alzheimer's cannot rob a thriving life of its ability to inspire, heal and complete. Your life is your gift from God; how you live your life is your gift to God. Moses, at age 120, is reported to have said to all of Israel:

> I call Heaven and Earth to record this day against you, that I have set before you life and death, blessing and cursing: therefore choose life, that both thou and thy seed may live. (Deuteronomy 30:19, KJV)

The answers to "Where will you live?" and "How will you pay for it?" must be in place before the *READY OR NOT* transition if they are to be effective. Likewise, attitudes and habits of character must be in place early on for you to thrive right to the end of life, and indeed for life during all of aging to have quality and meaning. As Warren Buffet put it, "The chains of habit are too light to be felt until they are too heavy to be broken." It seems paradoxical—but it is true—that present attention to the quality of the last stages of living not only determines the quality of the end of your life, it also determines the quality of your life right now.

From Control to Engagement

Let your mind play a little with an image of dancing with life. Dancing is a way of expressing yourself; dancing is thoughtful; dancing is romantic; dancing engages you with others; and dancing lifts you up out of yourself. Dancing takes balance and dancing takes music. But when you are really dancing it is as though effort disappears and you are moved by the music of the spheres. At age 85 Florida Scott-Maxwell danced her life literally and figuratively:

> My kitchen linoleum is so black and shiny that I waltz while I wait for the kettle to boil.[3]

It is not always this comfortable. The thought that you will no longer be in control of your own life in LIKE IT OR NOT and THE REST OF LIVING, when you are frail, terrifies most people. It may be this fear of loss of control that drives some people to say, "If it comes to that, I'll kill myself." A student in an adult development class expressed frustration with the idea of giving up control when she said, "I've worked very hard to be in control of my own life—and I've succeeded." Unfortunately, this is just an illusion! You can no more control life than a raft on white water can control the river. You can learn to work with the river—to dance with life—but you cannot control it.

Control originates from living a life grounded in fear. When life is lived on that basis, what is required is survival. And what is required for survival is control. There can be no authentic expression of the self, or embracing of others, when you live your life grounded in fear.

Think about what you can really control. Victor Frankl got it right when he reflected on what he and his fellow survivors of Nazi death camps experienced. It is hard to imagine a situation in which people had more reason to fear, or had less control. Yet what he found was that people who had an inner sense of purpose or meaning survived; those who did not were broken. Real control is not about controlling—it is about going with what is there. As you learn from the martial arts, the secret is not to try to control others by brute force, but to use the energy that is there to your advantage.

Those who thrive no longer push and pull at life in some great tug of war. People who are living their lives fully have gone beyond spending whatever energy they have insisting that the world operate on their terms—the weather, the traffic, their children, their job. Life is, indeed, what happens when you've made other plans.

As we have said, living beautifully and passionately with integrity and commitment—thriving—is possible right to life's last breath, even when that breath follows physical or mental deterioration. This may be surprising, but it is so, although thriving cannot be a last minute choice.

One way of assuring that you thrive is to distinguish the object of attention. On the one hand, this means attention to yourself and who you are and what you are called to be and do. This is normally referred to as self-expression, or expressing self. On the other hand, it means paying attention to how you relate to, or embrace, others.

When looked at in the context of attitudes toward and habits of the body, mind, heart and soul, this can give you clarity about what is required *now* to put in place habits that will free you to thrive. Life-sustaining practices of expressing self and embracing others are the two essential skills for thriving. They are worked out in four domains: body, mind, heart, and soul.

At the same time, we want to avoid any sense of fragmentation. You are one person. We affirm that. But we also know that when you talk about yourself you say things like, "I feel great. That workout made my day," or "I want some stimulating adult conversation," or "I'm on edge—work is getting to me," or "I need to be sure about what is important to me and what is not." In each of these you say "I"—you refer to yourself. But "I feel great. That workout made my day" points to you as a physical self. "I want some stimulating adult conversation" points to you as a thinking self. "I'm on edge—work is getting to me" points to you as a feeling self, and "I need to be sure about what is important to me and what is not" points to you as a spiritual self. When we speak, then, about thriving in body, mind, heart and spirit, we are speaking about you, yourself. But we focus on dimensions of who you are in order to get a full picture of what it means to thrive for all your life.

In what follows, you will learn how thriving kinds of self-expression and relationship to others work in these four domains. The first two, body and mind, are mostly about how you relate to and express yourself, although there are elements of embracing others in both. The second two, heart and soul, are complimentary. They tend to be more about embracing others, although there are aspects of expressing self in both.

---

1. Dorothy Field, PhD, "Looking back, what period of life brought you the most satisfaction." in *International Journal of Aging and Human Development*, 45 (6), 1997, 169-194.

2. www.grannyD.com; 4/29/99

3. Florida Scott-Maxwell, *The Measure of My Days*, New York: Penguin, 1979, p 28.

CHAPTER THIRTEEN

Thriving in Body and Mind

THE BODY

To talk positively about aging and physical decline goes against everything our culture teaches about aging. We are culturally conditioned to avoid positive thoughts of the body if it is not young, fit, and beautiful.

How we value antiquity does not translate to people. Old is good, even great, if you are talking about music, a palace, wine, literature, or furniture. ("Stood the test of time, you know!") Old is not so good when you start talking about people. Cultural conditioning gets right down to your core. Let's face it—where do your eyes want to rest if the choice is between two octogenarians and two 20-somethings, regardless of gender? In the middle years, it is not uncommon to sneak a glance at an older person and mentally shudder. Secretly, you are taking the measure of your own future. From the vantage point of feeling content about who you are now, it may look like you have a lot to lose. But those who are old have something to teach us.

When it comes to humans, young-looking, physically fit, and sexually attractive is "where it's at." Learning to appreciate a less glamorous body, in spite of cultural conditioning, is one of the elements of thriving.

At one level, the focus on young and virile and sexy makes an enormous amount of sense. These attributes are the mechanisms of preservation of the species. But physical preservation of the species is fundamentally a task of youth. At a time when life expectancy has been extended to almost a century, an inability to measure yourself in terms other than what is appropriate for youth will inhibit and prevent thriving. If you fully live your whole life, no matter how healthy you are, you will have to live a portion of it without the body of youth—without the looks, without the strength, and without the speed and physical flexibility.

Certainly, paying attention to exercise and nutrition pays dividends in terms of well-being. Pianist Arthur Rubenstein continued world-class concert performances into his eighties—because he practiced more than he had when he was younger to keep his hands and fingers flexible. The challenge is to be fully alive no matter what your physical condition is—to be fully alive exactly as you are and exactly as you are not. The task is to separate your sense of well-being from unnatural expectations, and to sustain a sense of personal wholeness in whatever condition your condition is in.

Any other understanding of the whole of a human life dishonors being old, and you cannot thrive in a condition that you do not honor. If the only way to be old is to be young, you have set yourself up for failure. It is a standard of OK-ness that is not sustainable.

When the Beatles asked, "Will you still love me, when I'm 64?" they were on to something critical. It's easy to love someone (including yourself) when everything is going perfectly. Love, including self-love, gets tested when "for better or worse, richer or poorer, in sickness and in health" does not mean—as Goldie Hawn once said on Laugh-In—"I'll take better, richer, and healthier."

Here's one person who will challenge that youth-oriented perspective. The New York Times reports in its "Metropolitan Diary:"

> I am retired and work as a volunteer at a hospital in southern New Jersey. The other day, as I started to leave the hospital elevator, a frail and very elderly visitor with a walker crossed the lobby. I held the door open and patiently waited. She slowly but determinedly shuffled into the elevator. As she did, she looked up at me, smiled and said, "I am sorry I took so long, but I'm breaking in a new pair of shoes."[1]

In late life, if you have learned to dance with life, you will still be able to embrace your body as the link between your inner and outer worlds, the vessel for expressing yourself and embracing others. We are not just referring to the physical tasks of getting through the day. Marc Kaminsky speaks in poetry about his grandmother, Esther Schwartzman:

> How can she tell her daughter
> What kind of man he became when
> Company left and for her alone
> He was a man of holidays.
> There was no night when he did not
> Take her into his arms and play with her
> For hours, before going to sleep.
> And people thought they went to bed early
> Because they were old.[2]

Probably the most unthinkable fate for any person in the middle years is to be old, frail, in a nursing home—and to wear diapers. Yet even in that place, even in that condition, some will not deny who they are. Some will thrive, and be fully alive, even when others might think their situation is degrading. This is how Anna Mae Halgrim Seaver dances with life in the semiprivacy of a nursing home where she is a resident—with trenchant wit and humor. About her day she writes:

> Let's watch a little TV. Oprah and Phil and Heraldo and who cares if some transvestite is having trouble picking a color-coordinated wardrobe from his husband's girlfriend's mother's collection. Lunch. Can't wait. Dried something with pureed peas and coconut pudding. No wonder I'm losing weight.[3]

Because she has accepted her limits and has freedom to embrace herself on her own terms, Anna Mae Halgrim Seaver is able to be amused—and amusing—about a state of affairs that would shame many:

> I don't much like some of the physical things that happen to us. I don't care much for a diaper. I seem to have lost the control acquired so diligently as a child. The difference is that I'm aware and embarrassed but I can't do anything about it. I've had three children and I know it isn't pleasant to clean another's diaper. My husband used to wear a gas mask when he changed the kids. I wish I had one now.[4]

We asked a group of physically frail people how they could laugh so much. Their reply was, "We have to laugh. We're pathetic, you know." There was neither putdown in this response, nor coyness, nor artifice. These people were comfortable to be themselves, just as they were. They were able to look out for themselves and for each other because they were able to look at themselves and each other with amused eyes and without flinching. And laugh.

1. When—at what age—did you feel most comfortable with your body? Why then? What is different now?

2. What one step can you take today to love your body even a little bit more, exactly as you are and exactly as you are not?

Will you do it? Please?

3. What one thing could you do—what piece of equipment could you get, what practice could you undertake, what attitude could you adjust—to compensate just a little bit better for the condition your condition is in?

Will you do it? Please?

THE MIND

The key to developing and maintaining the kinds of attitudes about your body that will sustain you when your body is no longer "perfect" will be your habits of appreciating it and compensating for its limitations. Arthur Rubinstein not only practiced more as he aged, he also played using variations and contrasts in speed to generate the impression of faster play. Developing those habits will be a function of how well you maintain your ability to focus on process rather than remembering results.

If your thinking stays flexible, you can adjust to your increasingly stiff body. In her famous poem, *Warning*, Jenny Joseph talks about more than just wearing purple. More importantly, she sees herself as a woman who will not be bound in later life by the social solutions she lives with now. Her playful spirit will emerge; she will explore new behaviors. Now, she must "set a good example for the children;" when she is old she imagines she will buy "brandy and summer gloves and satin sandals" even if it means she has to say she has no money to pay for groceries.[5]

Some people get "hardening of the attitudes" as early as EXTENDED MIDDLE AGE. We are not talking about people who were closed-minded all their lives. They have their own problems, which aging will not solve. We are talking about people who seemed in their middle years to be mentally flexible and adaptable but who, in late life, use old answers to new questions.

You may have heard the saying, "If I give you a fish, you can eat today, but if I teach you to fish, you can eat forever." The task for the mind in thriving is to keep fishing. Old catches that are kept indefinitely turn bad, and even start to stink.

A familiar example: a man in his forties wears a certain type of clothes, with distinguishing logos on the breast pockets. He sports a certain type of sunglasses, and favors certain colors. He looks great. He has figured out how to dress to his best advantage, and to project an image that tells you who he is and how he stands in the world. But, if he continues to wear the same garb thirty or forty years later, what happens? He will look foolish, out of touch, out of step. Even if his clothes look new and expensive, they will be inappropriate because they will make a statement about what was, not what is. He solved a problem of how he wanted to appear to others when he was in his forties; in his seventies and eighties he retained the solution, but lost the process.

Part of growing up is learning to deal with real, concrete problems and developing workable solutions in many arenas, such as work, home, and relationships. What can happen, however, is this: in the height of the middle years, you address these complex, concrete problems successfully. You come to a sense of mastery and control. The successful solving of problems makes you feel good about yourself and the solutions you have come to, and may even contribute significantly to career success. Having solutions becomes part of expressing yourself.

And there's the hook! The solutions get poured in concrete. You come to rely on the solutions rather than on the process of getting to the solutions, whether the solutions are still appropriate or not. You can lose—more likely, misplace—the flexibility and creativity that got you to the solutions and made you successful. You have stopped fishing, and are just hanging on to the old fish.

What you need to learn is to be suspicious that what "always" worked might not serve you any more. You need to be able to use your experience and knowledge as guideposts pointing in a direction, rather than road signs along a certain well-worn path (that may be a rut). Learn to look for habitual thoughts, and to develop a joyful way of challenging assumptions (especially your own!). Not only will the exercise be good for your mental strength, it will keep you stimulated and interested in all the wonderful and not so wonderful developments in the world around you.

Being with people of any age who are dogmatic, opinionated, or passively closed-minded is wearying. It sucks the life out of relationships, even as the defensiveness of it signals the loss of self-expression that accompanies it. It is so much work to be around people like that. There is no give and take; it's all "I give, you take." It is more like wrestling than dancing, and there is no thriving in that.

Before you roll your eyes at your elders and swear you won't be like those who are closed-minded, think about this. "Middle rather than old age is probably the time when mental flexibility becomes a critical issue, for it is in the middle years that most people have attained their peak status, when they feel they have worked out a sense of answers to life, and when, at least in some ways, they may forgo strenuous effort to envision new or different patterns of thought and action."[6]

Right now, whether you are in middle age or beyond it, you are challenged to be mentally flexible, focusing on process rather than once-and-for all solutions. You need to be certain to act in ways that reinforce your rock-solid commitment to thriving and fully living the rest of your life. A key part of that is mental flexibility.

1. What are some core values that you never want to change (such as, "My family will always come first" or "It is wrong to waste money.")?

2. List three important—but not eternal—solutions you have used to embody one or another of your values (such as, "My family gathers at my home every Christmas," or "I won't stay in any hotel that costs more than $49 per night.")

3. Is there another way to express or embody any of your core values that might work better today?

[1] "Metropolitan Diary," *The New York Times*, March 2, 1998, p. A18.
[2] "Erev Shabbos," in *Daily Bread*, University of Illinois Press, Urbana, IL, 1982. p. 23.
[3] "My World Now," *Newsweek*, June 27, 1994, p. 11.
[4] *Ibid.*
[5] Jenny Joseph, "Warning," in Sandra Martz, Ed., *When I Am an Old Woman I Shall Wear Purple*, Watsonville, CA: Papier-Maché Press, 1991, p. 1.
[6] Robert F. Peck and Howard Berkowitz, "Personality and Adjustment in Middle Age." In Bernice L. Neugarten and Associates (Eds.), *Personality in Middle and Late Life, Empirical Studies*. New York: Prentice-Hall/Atherton Press, 1964, p. 17.

CHAPTER FOURTEEN

Thriving in Heart and Soul

THE HEART

The domain of the heart includes the human capacity to love, to be empathetic, and to invest strong meaningful emotion in the lives of others. What is at stake in late life is this: if you are privileged to grow old, you are likely to outlive some of your friends and lovers. You may even bury some of your children. If you have grandchildren, they will grow up and often will move away—at least they will no longer be the lovely little children with whom you took a walk in the park, or to the pond to feed the ducks.

Activities in which you invested yourself in your younger years (work, bridge groups, church circles, travel, volunteering) may no longer be available because of real physical limitations or because you are stuck in ways of thinking that no longer support those activities. For example, we know a woman who had been an active traveler with her husband, but who stopped traveling altogether after his death. When asked why, her response was, "I can't check into a hotel by myself. That is a man's job!"

The domain of the heart also stands for the ability to value your self for your personal atttributes, and not to rely entirely on one or two life roles (such as parent, grandparent, spouse, worker, athlete, lover) for self-identity. Who you see yourself to be is in part formed from relationships in which you have a role. These roles give you a sense of self-worth, enjoyment, meaning, and identity. But in the end you are more than simply the sum of your roles.

Emotional agility means that you are able to value and express yourself, even apart from roles to which you have been deeply attached. Part of the challenge of thriving in the domain of the heart is to move from an identity based on your roles to an identity based on your existence. It is to move from knowing yourself by what you do to knowing yourself by who you are.

Your circle of friends and relatives begins to be broken by death and choices you or they make about where to live. The world of people and activities, in which and through which you embraced others and expressed yourself in strong meaningful relationships, shrinks.

Picture your world as a small town, late in the evening. Lights go out one at a time. At first—*click*—while each light is missed, the town is not dark and you are not alone—*click*. But as more and more lights blink out—*click, click*—the world grows dark. This is a late-life, grown-up version of the childhood terror of being—*click*—alone in the dark, but now the dark is the darkness of the heart— *click, click, click*. You can yell "Mommy" all you want, but it won't matter.

You will simply suffer an increasingly impoverished emotional life if you are unable to invest your emotions in other people and pursuits. There is no way to stop lights from going out, but you can always turn on new lights. So, the challenge of the heart in late life is this: to learn to embrace new people with meaningful commitments of emotion, and to move in new circles to make new contacts. It is to learn to sing as heartfelt a song at midnight as you did at noon.

This might not appear to be the "natural" flow of life. Relationships should, it seems, be formed when there is young energy to spark them. There is some truth to this and that truth is expressed when you hear things such as, "old friends are best friends" and "blood is thicker than water." But there is only *some* truth to it.

In the previous chapter you learned about the need to keep your mind agile, and not to get stuck on patterns of action that are the products of long-forgotten thought processes. In the domain of the heart, the issue is emotional agility. Being emotionally agile is not the same as being an emotional flit. Rather, the challenge is to let go of psychological attachments when your loved ones are no longer there, and to be willing to take the risk to reach out for new relationships as opportunities appear. Emotional agility is about being invested in people who can respond, instead of people who are gone. As hard as it may feel to acknowledge this, the truth is that as long as you are thriving, neither the presence nor the absence of any other person can destroy personal meaning. The responsibility of those of us who are left alive is to continue to live. And to thrive is to be in relationship with other living things.

An Invitation to Friendship

1. In the diagram below, put at least five people in each circle, with those closest to you nearest the center.

1.

2.

3.

4.

5.

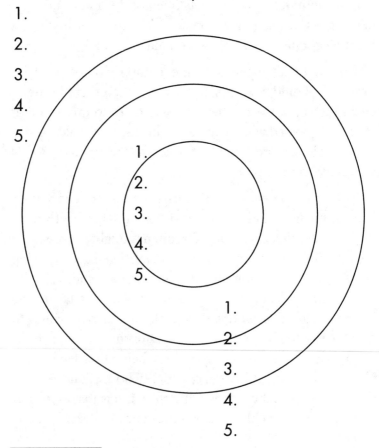

2. Now, put beside each person's name the number of years you have known him or her.

3. Choose one or two people you may wish to invite to move one circle closer in your friendship.

4. Who else would you like to invite into one of the circles?

The Soul

This brings us to the last domain in which thriving finds expression—the soul, or spirit. In the domain of the body, the challenge is to express your self with your body exactly as it is and exactly as it is not. In the domain of the mind, the challenge is to express your self without succumbing to mental rigidity or inactivity. The challenges for heart and soul are focused on reaching out to others. In the case of the soul, this reaching out is to touch the core of the mystery of life. For some, this is "ultimate meaning," for others "the sacred" or "the divine." For many, it is simply God.

Florida Scott Maxwell, on Easter Sunday of her 85th year, figured it this way: "Easter Day. I am in that rare frame of mind when everything seems simple. When I have no doubt that the aim and solution of life is the acceptance of God. It is impossible and imperative, and clear… I am where the mystery is the certainty."[1]

For some, to be "where the mystery is the certainty" is to be religious in a worshipful or denominational sense. If you have long been involved in the life of a congregation, the poignant part of life might find you changing your relationship to what has been both your source of strength and your way of serving others. For some, it may be time to look to the congregation more for support and spiritual nurturance than as an opportunity to serve. The movement from ritual and service to a more intensely personal relationship with God can be described as religious maturity. Jane Marie Thibault captures the possible depth of a new way of being with the sacred in the title of her book, *A Deepening Love Affair With God*.

At one level, it makes sense to us that, as the senses grow dim and as time spent alone grows longer, you may reach out to the One you have always known as the source of all Love. But what if your memory, consciousness, and intellect—your mental faculties—grow dark? Science simply does not know, even in great mental darkening, what is happening in the depths of the self. But what may be happening there is a powerfully connected level of being.

> For night music is the song of the unconscious, that web of patterns and connections woven in the rich underground world of evolution and history, the collective memory of non-living as well as living beings, that mite of matter through which all of creation shares spirit. Night music melts the separateness of subjectivity and prepares the soul for deep communion.[2]

Humans do not have adequate or well-understood words to describe a spiritual self that has transcended the human self. Even the dark night of the spirit may find you reaching out to embrace and be embraced by love. What is certain is that it is a mystery. The domain of the spirit does not submit to empirical measurement or to scientific method. It does not submit to knowing in the same way you know other things.

For some, to be where the mystery is the certainty does not use an explicitly religious vocabulary. Nevertheless, the goal is the same. A sense of this is captured in the book title *Out of the Skin, Into the Soul: The Art of Aging*. The authors explain:

But many can identify some moment more than any other when the reality of aging became a more permanent life fixture, and with it, the need to create new meanings for the self, to bring a rich and chaotic past to bear on the present moments, and to sense some renewed significance for the future.[3]

For all, to be where the mystery is the certainty is to be at a place in life where one explores the possibility of reaching out to embrace love. As T. S. Eliot puts it:

Love is most nearly itself
When here and now cease to matter.
Old men ought to be explorers
Here and there does not matter
We must be still and still moving
Into another intensity
For a further union, a deeper communion…
In my end is my beginning.[4]

To be where the mystery is the certainty may also be the key to thriving throughout life. To stand where the mystery is the certainty is to stand in love, and what is available there is thriving. Standing in love, free of the need to try to control life for survival's sake, what is available is satisfaction with who you are as one who is in the presence of the sacred. What is available is genuine expression of the self, and generosity for embracing others. To stand where the mystery is the certainty is to dance with living as life comes at you, foregoing a need to control it, in exchange for the exuberance of the journey. It is to thrive, and to fully live. When control is exposed as impossible, as it is in the inevitable diminishments of aging, to live where the mystery is the certainty is be able to fully live the rest of your life.

It is also to be at peace with dying. We don't know about you, but dying runs in our families. What sets the domain of the spirit apart from the domains of body, mind, and heart is that the spirit transcends even death. For many, the next life becomes and is as real as this life. People do not die, they pass over to the other side. For others, even of the old, the sureness of eternal life is less strong. But even for them, there can be faith that in death they will never be lost to the loving memory of God. Henry's Uncle Austin put it in his own words at the end of his life: "I figure it this way. When you are born, you are taken into loving, welcoming arms. When you die, can it be any less?"

For us, there is no expressing of the self or embracing of the other that adequately measures the beauty of the human spirit without also affirming the Divine Spark within. What is called for in living is thriving, and that is true regardless of age or place on the journey of life.

Aging happens. How it happens is the variable, and the experience you have of it is, in large measure, up to you. We invite you to fully live, and to thrive, right through it.

---

[1] Florida Scott-Maxwell, *The Measure of My Days*, New York: Penguin, 1979, pp. 106-107.

[2] Dorothy Albracht Dougherty and Mary Colgan McNamara, *Out of the Skin, Into the Soul: The Art of Aging*, San Diego, CA: LuraMedia, 1993, p. 42.

[3] *Ibid.*, p. 67.

[4] T. S. Eliot, "East Coker," *Four Quartets*, London: Faber and Faber, 1944, pp. 31-32.

Suggested Reading List

AGING

✧ Booth, Wayne. *The Art of Growing Older: Writers on Living and Aging.* Chicago: The University of Chicago Press, 1996.

✧ Carter, Jimmy. *The Virtues of Aging.* New York: Ballantine, 1998.

✧ Cole, Thomas R. and Sally Gadow, eds. *What Does It Mean To Grow Old: Reflections From the Humanities.* Durham, NC: Duke University Press, 1986.

✧ Cole, Thomas R. and Mary G. Winkler, eds. *The Oxford Book of Aging.* New York: Oxford University Press, 1994.

✧ Nearing, Helen. *Light on Aging and Dying.* New York: Harcourt Brace & Co., 1997.

✧ Roszak, Theodore. *America the Wise: The Longevity Revolution and the True Wealth of Nations.* Boston, MA: Houghton Mifflin & Co., 1998.

✧ Rowe, John W., M.D., and Robert L. Kahn, Ph.D. *Successful Aging.* New York: Dell, 1999.

WHERE WILL YOU LIVE?

✧ American Association of Homes and Services for the Aging (AAHSA). *The Consumer's Directory of Continuing Care Retirement Communities.* Washington, DC, 1997.

✧ Frolik, Lawrence A. *Residence Options for Older or Disabled Clients* Boston, MA: Warren, Gorham and Lamont, 1999.

✧ Porcino, Jane. *Living Longer, Living Better: Adventures in Community Housing For Those in the Second Half of Life.* New York: Continuum, 1991.

✧ Wasch, William K. *Home Planning for Your Later Years,* Middltown, CT: Independence Resource Center, 1996.

HOW WILL YOU PAY FOR IT?

✣ Shilling, Dana *Financial Planning for the Older Client, 4th Edition*. Cincinnati, OH: National Underwriter, 1999.

✣ Clifford, Dennis, Esq. and Cora Jordan, Esq. *Plan Your Estate*, Berkeley, CA: Nolo Press, 1998.

HOW WILL YOU LIVE?

✣ Bianchi, Eugene C. *Elder Wisdom: Crafting Your Own Elderhood*, New York: Crossroad, 1994.

✣ Bianchi, Eugene C. *Aging As A Spiritual Journey*. New York: Crossroad, 1982.

✣ Doherty, Dorothy Albracht and Mary Colgan McNamara. *Out of the Skin, Into the Soul: The Art of Aging*. SanDiego, CA: Lura-Media, 1993.

✣ Frankl, Viktor E. *Man's Search for Meaning: An Introduction to Logotherapy*. New York: Simon & Shuster, 1984.

✣ Gray, Ruth Howard, *Survival of the Spirit: My Detour Through a Retirement Home*. Atlanta, GA: John Knox Press, 1985.

✣ Nouwen, Henri J. M., and Walter J. Gaffney. *Aging: The Fulfillment of Life*, New York: Doubleday, 1974.

✣ Oliver, Gene. *Life and the Art of Change*. Costa Mesa,CA: LifeChange Press, 1998.

✣ Scott-Maxwell, Florida. *The Measure of My Days*. New York: Penguin, 1968.

✣ Thibault, Jane Marie. *A Deepening Love Affair: the Gift of God in Later Life*. Nashville, TN: Upper Room, 1993.

Index

About the Authors

Henry C. Simmons, Ph.D., is Professor of Religion and Aging and Director of the Center on Aging at Union Theological Seminary and Presbyterian School of Christian Education in Richmond, VA. He is a Charter Fellow of the Association for Gerontology in Higher Education, an ordained minister, and a nationally known teacher on religion and aging.

E. Craig MacBean is the founder and a Managing Member of PrimeDynamics, LLC—a company dedicated to the possibility of thriving throughout aging. He sits on the Board of Directors of The National Council on the Aging, Inc. (NCOA) and the National Institute on Financial Issues and Services for Elders (NIFSE). Long active in the life and health insurance industry, Craig is an authority on the financial dynamics of aging.